GUY FAWKES;

OR,

A COMPLETE HISTORY
OF
THE GUNPOWDER TREASON,

A.D. 1605;
WITH
A DEVELOPEMENT OF THE PRINCIPLES OF THE
CONSPIRATORS,
AND
SOME NOTICES OF THE REVOLUTION OF 1688.
BY THE
REV. THOMAS LATHBURY, M.A.,
Author of "A History of the English Episcopacy, from 1640 to 1662,"
and "The State of Popery and Jesuitism in England from the
Reformation, till 1829."

PREFACE.

Though the particulars connected with the Gunpowder Treason may be perused in the general histories of the period, yet I am not aware, that any modern narrative of that dark design is to be found in a separate form. Many brief sketches have, indeed, been published in various modern works: but no full and complete history of the Treason has ever been set forth. In compiling the present volume, I have collected, from various quarters, all the information which I could discover on the subject. It will be found to be the most complete narrative of the Treason ever published in a detached form: at the same time it is sufficiently concise not to weary the patience of the reader.

As to the seasonableness of such a publication, there can be but one opinion among Churchmen. The aspect of the times, the rapid advances of Romanism, the appointment of certain Roman Catholics to high and important offices in the State, and the countenance given to Popery in high places, are circumstances which naturally direct the attention of all reflecting persons to the principles of that Church, which has recently appeared to gain fresh strength in this country. The question must force itself upon the notice of every true Protestant. The Church of England is assailed on every side, simply because she is the strongest bulwark ever erected against the encroachments of Popery: and history proves that, from the period of the Reformation, our own Church has been unceasingly attacked, in some way or other, by the advocates of Romanism. It is, therefore, very desirable that we should consult the past history of our country, in order that we may discover how the active emissaries of Rome have always acted. The Gunpowder Treason is one of the darkest tragedies in our domestic history: and the present work contains a faithful narrative of that detestable conspiracy. I have endeavoured also to exhibit the principles on which the conspirators acted: and I have proved that these principles are still retained by the Church of Rome.

In order to furnish the reader with a full view of the working of Popish principles, I have given a sketch of all the Papal attempts against Queen Elizabeth.

In the last chapter I have inserted the Act of Parliament for the Observance of the Fifth of November. I have printed the Act, because there are many clergymen who have never seen it, and who are not acquainted with the few works in which it is to be found. The clergy are commanded to read this Act every year, on the Fifth of November: and as it is not easily to be procured, or, at all events, is not attainable in a separate form, I cannot but conceive that I am performing an acceptable service, in thus placing it before the public. It is my earnest hope that the publication of this little volume may be the means of bringing some of my clerical brethren to a better observance of the day.

I have also noticed the variations which the Service for the Fifth of November has undergone, since its first publication in 1606, to its final revision in 1689.

It is true that every one knows something of the history of the Gunpowder Treason: but it is also true, that very few are acquainted with those principles which gave it birth. We see, in this treason, to what lengths the principles of the Church of Rome have led their votaries: and who can assert that she is, in any respect, changed? The Romanist denies that the principles of his Church are changed: nay, he must do so, or renounce the doctrine of infallibility, which is incompatible with change: why, then, should Protestants volunteer assertions, respecting the altered character of Popery, when the Papists themselves deny the fact altogether? I may venture to assert that the individual who advances such a statement, is ignorant of the real principles of the Church of Rome.

Bath,
October, 1839.

CHAPTER I.

A SKETCH OF PAPAL ATTEMPTS IN ENGLAND AND IRELAND
DURING THE REIGN OF ELIZABETH. THE STATE OF
RELIGION AND THE COUNTRY ON JAMES'S ACCESSION.

As an introduction to the subject, of which this volume professes more especially to treat, I purpose to give a sketch of the proceedings of the emissaries of Rome in this country, during the long reign of Queen Elizabeth. Queen Mary died A.D. 1558, when her sister Elizabeth succeeded her on the throne. Paul IV. at this time occupied the papal chair: but in less than a year after her accession he was removed by death, and was succeeded by Pius IV. Both these pontiffs were quiet and moderate men, compared with several of those who came after them. At all events, they did not proceed to those extremities to which their successors resorted. There were, indeed, parties in the court of Rome, who laboured to induce these pontiffs to excommunicate the queen, as a heretic and a usurper; but recollecting the fatal consequences which had issued from the hasty proceedings of Clement against Henry VIII., or, probably imagining that greater benefits would result from gentle than from violent measures, they pursued a moderate course, exhorting the queen to return to her allegiance to the see of Rome, and even making promises of concessions respecting the reformation. In 1566, Pius V. was promoted to the papal chair. In a very brief space he gave indications of a departure from the moderate councils of his two immediate predecessors. The efforts of Philip II. of Spain were also, during the early years of this reign, directed to the same object with those of Paul IV. and Pius IV. The king was anxious to marry Elizabeth, in order that he might exercise his influence in England; and as long as he could entertain a hope that his wishes would be realized, he seconded the moderate measures of the Roman pontiff. His expectations on this subject were destined to disappointment; when perceiving that a marriage with the queen was out of the question, he directed his attention towards the accomplishment of his designs on this country by other means than those of treaty and diplomacy.

As soon as Pius V. was fixed in the papal chair a different line of policy, therefore, was pursued towards England. Some few years, indeed, elapsed before the queen was actually excommunicated; but conspiracies and treasons were contrived at Rome, with a view to their execution, as soon as suitable persons could be found for the purpose.

Pius V. was the pontiff by whom the bull of excommunication against Elizabeth was issued. The document was dated March, 1569, or 1570, according to the present mode of computation. Hitherto the court of Rome had abstained from any direct attempt against the queen and the country: but from this time plots were contrived and treasons planned in rapid succession; for when one scheme was frustrated, by the vigilance of the government, another was adopted; so that the whole reign of Elizabeth, with the exception of the early portion of it, was constantly developing some machination or other, devised by the emissaries of Rome. At the head of the confederacy against the queen were the pope and the king of Spain, who hated her with the most deadly hatred,—the former, because she was the chief stay of the reformation, the latter, because she was an obstacle to the prosecution of his designs on this country[1].

The first act of rebellion was the attempt of the earls of Westmoreland and Northumberland. This was soon after the bull was issued. In all the treasons and rebellions of this reign some of the priests of Rome were more or less concerned; and these two earls were instigated to the attempt by Morton, an Englishman and a priest, who was sent into England by the pope himself, for the express purpose of

---

[1] I subjoin a few extracts from the bull issued against Elizabeth. It was entitled *The Damnation and Excommunication of Queen Elizabeth.* It commenced thus: "He that reigneth on high committed one Holy, Catholic, and Apostolic Church (out of which there is no salvation) to one alone upon earth, namely, to Peter, and to Peter's successor, the bishop of Rome. *Him alone he made prince over all people, and all kingdoms, to pluck up, destroy, scatter, consume, plant, and build, that he may contain the faithful that are knit together with the band of charity, in the unity of the Spirit.*" Then, after an enumeration of Elizabeth's alleged crimes against the holy see, his holiness proceeds: "We do, out of the fulness of our apostolic power, declare the aforesaid Elizabeth, being a heretic, and a favourer of heretics, to have incurred the sentence of *anathema*, and to be cut off from the unity of the body of Christ. And, moreover, *we do declare her to be deprived of her pretended title to the kingdom aforesaid, and of all dominion, dignity, and privilege.* And also the nobility, subjects, and people of the said kingdom, and all others, who have in any sort sworn unto her, *to be for ever absolved from any such oath.* And we do command and interdict all and every the noblemen, subjects, and people, *that they presume not to obey her, or her monitions, mandates, and laws.*"

It is necessary to give these extracts in the outset, in order that it may be seen that the gunpowder treason, and almost all other treasons in the reigns of Elizabeth and James, flowed from the doctrines thus promulgated by the papal see.

stirring up rebellion. This design, however, was strangled in its birth, and its promoters paid the penalty of their lives.

In 1576 Pius V. paid the debt of nature, and was succeeded by Gregory XIII., who did not depart from the practices of his predecessor. Stukely, another subject of the queen's, was authorised to go into Ireland by his holiness and the king of Spain; and the pope had the presumption to pretend to confer the title of marquis and earl of several places in that country. He was commissioned to stir up rebellion, the pope engaging to supply men, and the king of Spain promising supplies of money. The purpose was, however, defeated: but the next year several individuals were actually sent into Ireland, accompanied, as usual, by Sanders, a priest, who was possessed with legantine authority from his holiness. To encourage the Irish, a banner, consecrated by the pope, was sent over, and every other means was resorted to, which the most inveterate enmity could devise. The pontiff also sent them his apostolical benediction, granting to all who should fall in the attempt against the *heretics*, a plenary indulgence for all their sins, and the same privileges as were conferred on those who fell in battle against the Turks. Sanders, however, died miserably, and the attempt completely failed.

It was about the year 1580 that the seminary priests, who were so designated from the circumstance of being trained in certain seminaries on the Continent, instituted especially for English priests, began to come over into England for the express purpose of enforcing the bull of excommunication against the queen. These men were natives of England, though educated on the Continent. They assumed various disguises on their arrival, travelling from place to place to promote the grand design, which had been projected at Rome. They endeavoured to execute the bull by making various attempts upon the queen's life, from which, however, she was mercifully delivered. Two points were constantly kept in view: the one to stir up dissensions at home, among the queen's subjects; the other to induce the papal sovereigns to promise men and arms, whenever it should be deemed desirable to make a descent on the country. Many of these men were executed as traitors, though the Romanists pretend that they were martyrs for their religion[2]. It is true that their religious views led them into treason and

[2] For a full discussion of the question, whether the priests and others who suffered death at this period and subsequently, were punished for religion or for treason, the author's work, *The State of Popery and Jesuitism in England*, may be consulted. In that work I have entered fully into the subject, and have proved that all the parties who suffered were executed for treason.

rebellion; yet they were no more martyrs for their faith than the murderer who was executed at Tyburn. Parsons and Campion were the leaders of this body: the former escaped to the Continent, the latter was taken and executed for his treasonable practices.

It is constantly asserted by Roman Catholic writers, that the priests who suffered during this reign were martyrs to the faith: and the inference is attempted to be drawn, that the church of England is as much exposed to the charge of persecution as the church of Rome. One thing is certain, however, that, whether the advisers of Elizabeth were justified in their course or otherwise, they did not consider that they were putting men to death for religion: but, on the other hand, the martyrs under Queen Mary were committed to the flames as heretics, not as traitors or offenders against the laws of the land. When, therefore, Romanist writers attempt to draw a parallel between the martyrs of the Anglican church under Queen Mary, and the priests who suffered in the reign of Elizabeth, it is a sufficient answer to their cavils to allege the fact, that the former were put to death according to the mode prescribed in cases of heresy, which was an offence against religion; the latter were tried and executed for treason, which is an offence against the state. It is the remark of Archbishop Tillotson that, "We have found by experience that ever since the reformation they have continually been pecking at the foundations of our peace and religion; when God knows we have been so far from thirsting after their blood, that we did not so much as desire their disquiet, but in order to our own necessary safety, and indeed to theirs."

In 1583 Somerville attempted to kill the queen. The plot was discovered, and its author only escaped a public execution by strangling himself in prison.

In 1585 another plot was revealed. Parry, who had been employed on the Continent, came into England with a fixed determination to take the life of the queen. To this act he was instigated by the pope, who sent him his benediction, with a plenary indulgence for his sins. He was discovered and condemned. On his trial he produced the pope's letter, which had been penned by one of the cardinals.

At this time, when it was found that all the plots were secretly contrived or supported by the seminary priests, certain severe statutes were enacted. The priests, whose only occupation in England was to stir up rebellion, were commanded to quit the country, or be subjected to the charge of treason. These enactments were absolutely necessary, for every priest was a traitor: nor was it possible that it should have been otherwise, where the pope himself encouraged them in their designs.

During this year Sixtus V. was elected pope in the room of Gregory XIII. This pontiff walked in the steps of his immediate predecessors. It should be stated, that at that time the doctrine was inculcated, that it was meritorious to kill heretics, and those who were excommunicated. To die, therefore, in any such attempts, as those to which I have alluded, was deemed the readiest way to the crown of martyrdom, which was coveted by many members of the church of Rome. When such doctrines were believed, we cannot be surprised that so many treasons and rebellions were contrived.

In 1586 the life of the queen was attempted by Babington. The plot was discovered, and he and several of his accomplices were executed.

Thus it became necessary to frame new laws to prevent the plots of the seminary priests, who flocked into England for the sole purpose of exciting rebellion. A statute was, therefore, passed, by which it was made treason for any one, who had been ordained a priest by authority of the see of Rome, since Elizabeth's accession, to come into her dominions. This act was charged with cruelty at the time, and the charge is still repeated, not only by Romanist, but by many other writers: yet the act was absolutely necessary in self-defence. It was intended to keep the priests out of the country, since their coming always issued in treason and the consequent loss of their lives. Let it be remembered that the laws against recusants were not enacted until the treasons of Campion, Parry, and others, had rendered such a step on the part of the government unavoidable. The course adopted to prevent the coming of the priests was a merciful one, for it was supposed that they would not venture into England at the peril of their lives: it was also a reasonable one, since no sovereign was ever known to permit men to reside in his dominions, who denied that he was the lawful prince, and who endeavoured to withdraw his subjects from their allegiance, or stir them up to rebellion. As early even as the reign of Edward I., to bring in a bull from Rome was adjudged to be treason[3].

---

[3] By the 27th Elizabeth, c. 2, it was enacted, "Because Jesuits, seminary priests, or other priests came over into this realm of England, of purpose, as it hath appeared by sundry of their own examinations and confessions,—not only to withdraw her highness's subjects from their due obedience, but also to stir up and move sedition, rebellion and open hostility—to the utter ruin, desolation, and overthrow of the whole realm, if the same be not the sooner by some good means foreseen and prevented, that it shall not be lawful for any Jesuit, seminary priest, or other such priest—being born within this realm— ordained by any authority derived from the see of Rome, to come into,

The next year a similar plot, which was devised by an Englishman of the name of Moody, was brought to light. All these attempts were directed against Elizabeth herself; and though Englishmen were the traitors, who engaged to carry the plots into execution, yet they were encouraged in their work, and supported both by the pope and the king of Spain. The intention of the papal party was to dethrone Elizabeth, and seat Mary, queen of Scots, on the throne. No one will justify Elizabeth in taking the life of Mary: but it may be observed that if no attempts had been made against the queen's life, and if the court of Rome had acted justly and honourably, the ministers of Elizabeth would never have recommended the execution of that unfortunate queen. Her death must be attributed to Romish principles, and to the papal attacks on the Protestant religion[4].

The year 1588 is memorable in English history for the defeat of the *Spanish Armada*, impiously called the *Invincible Armada*. Several years were occupied in its preparation; and the enemies of England expected to overwhelm the country by one stroke. At this time the pope issued another bull against the queen, in which it was pretended that she was deprived of her royal dignity and kingdom, while her subjects were absolved from their allegiance. The same document commands all Englishmen to unite with the Spaniards on their landing, and to submit themselves to the Spanish general. Ample rewards also are promised to any who shall deliver the *proscribed woman*, as she is termed, into the hands of the papal party; while a full pardon was granted to all who should engage in the enterprise. It was determined that King Philip should hold the kingdom *in fee* from the pope. To accomplish their purpose, the Armada was fitted out.

---

be, or remain in, any part of this realm: and if he do, that then every such offence shall be taken and adjudged to be high treason, and every person so offending shall for his offence be adjudged a traitor." This statute was rendered necessary by the treasonable practices of the priests. Had they not been engaged in such practices, the statute never would have been devised. The only way, in which it can be said, that such priests suffered for religion is this, namely, *that their religion led them into treason*; but this would be to charge all their sufferings upon the church of Rome herself, which is indeed the fact, though Romanists will not admit it.

[4] At this time Cardinal Allen, an Englishman, published a defence of Stanley's treason, maintaining that in consequence of the queen's excommunication and heresy, it was not only lawful, but a duty to deprive her of the kingdom.

Though King Philip was the individual, by whom the Armada was fitted out, yet he was encouraged in the designed invasion by the pope as well as by the English fugitives on the Continent, headed by Sir William Stanley. The war with Portugal had, for some years, prevented Philip from bending all his energies towards the conquest of England. Being successful in his attempts on his neighbours, and also in the East Indies, it was argued by his flatterers that equal success would attend his efforts against England. Nor was another argument forgotten as a spur to his diligence, namely, that the conquest of England, with the consequent re-establishment of popery, would be an acceptable service to God, who had given him his great success against his enemies, and that no action could be more meritorious. It is stated that a hundred *Monks* and *Jesuits* accompanied the expedition; while Cardinal Allen, an Englishman, was appointed superintendent of ecclesiastical affairs throughout England. After having suffered much from the fire of the English fleet, as well as from the violence of the tempests, many of their ships being disabled, it was determined to attempt to return home through the Northern Ocean. At this time the powder of the English fleet was almost exhausted; so that the departure of the Spanish vessels, at this juncture, must be regarded as an interposition of divine providence in favour of our country. Many of the vessels which thus escaped from the English fleet, never reached the coast of Spain, being wrecked in different places. Elizabeth displayed a most magnanimous spirit during the time that the Armada was hovering around our coasts. She addressed the army in terms calculated to inspire them with confidence, and to endear them to her person. A solemn fast had been observed when the danger threatened; and when the deliverance of the country was manifest, a solemn thanksgiving was offered up in St. Paul's Cathedral on the 8th of September, when some of the Spanish ensigns lately taken were hung about the church. On Sunday, September 24th, the queen herself proceeded to St. Paul's, and on arriving at the west door, she knelt down within the church, and in an audible voice praised God as her only defender against her enemies. It was further ordered that the 19th of November should be observed as a day of thanksgiving throughout the country; which day was annually commemorated during the reign of Elizabeth[5].

In 1590, Urban VII. became pope. He was succeeded in a very brief space by Gregory XIV., who also was speedily succeeded by

---

[5] Several medals were stamped in commemoration of the defeat. One bore this inscription, under a fleet flying with full sails, *Venit, vidit, fugit*: another the following, *Dux Fœmina facti*. Several medal were also stamped in the Low Countries.

Innocent IX. Nor did Innocent occupy the papal chair for any lengthened period. In consequence of the defeat of the *Armada*, and also of the rapid changes in the holy see, three popes having died within the space of eighteen months, there was a slight cessation from the attempts against Elizabeth. In 1592, Clement VIII. was elevated to the popedom: and under his auspices there was a revival of the previous practices, which had not been given up, but merely relinquished for a season. During the years 1592, 1593, and 1594, several persons were commissioned by the court of Rome to raise rebellions in England, and to poison or assassinate the queen. The watchful eye of providence, however, was extended over the country and the queen. Every plot was discovered; every hostile design failed; and the only sufferers were the traitors themselves.

Patrick Cullen received absolution and the sacrament, A.D. 1592, from the Jesuit Holt, by whom it was determined to be a meritorious deed to kill the queen; and in 1594, Williams and York came over to England for the same purpose, having first received the sacrament in the Jesuits' college. In the year 1597, Squire came over from Spain with the same object in view, namely, the assassination of the queen; he also was instigated by Walpole, a *Jesuit*, from whom he received the sacrament under a promise to put the project in execution, and then conceal the deed. It was observed by Sir Edward Coke, that since the Jesuits set foot in England, there never passed four years without a pernicious treason.

About this time the English fleet obtained a most decisive victory over the Spanish. In 1598, Philip of Spain, the great enemy of England, was removed by death from that scene, in which he had, for so many years, acted so conspicuous, yet inglorious a part.

In 1599 and 1600, a rebellion was headed in Ireland by Tir Owen. This rebel chief was, as usual, encouraged by the pope, who sent him a plume of feathers as a token of his favour.

In 1603, the queen died in peace. From the preceding abstract it will appear, that from the year 1570 to 1600, Queen Elizabeth and the Protestant religion were constantly exposed to the machinations of the active partisans of the Roman see, who were encouraged by the pope himself. Every pontiff pursued the same course. There was a settled purpose at Rome, and, indeed, throughout the whole Romish confederacy, to dethrone Elizabeth and overturn the Anglican church; nor is it a libel on the church of Rome to say, that in all these proceedings, she acted on recognised principles—principles which had received the solemn sanction of her councils. To root out heresy, by any means within their reach, was deemed, or at all events was asserted to be a sacred duty incumbent on all the members of the church of

Rome. The doctrine may be denied in the present day, when times and circumstances do not permit of its being carried into practice; but, unquestionably, it was not merely believed as an article of faith in the days of Elizabeth, for we have seen that the attempt was made to enforce the bull which was issued against the queen.

James I. succeeded to the throne at a period when the eyes of Romanists were fastened on England as their prey. During the latter years of Elizabeth, the emissaries of Rome were comparatively quiet, in the hope that James, from a feeling of filial reverence towards the memory of his unfortunate mother, would not be unfavourably disposed towards their church. It is certain, however, that a plot was in agitation before the death of Elizabeth, being managed by some of those individuals who were impatient of waiting the course of events on the queen's death. The confessions and examinations of the conspirators show that the powder plot was partly contrived before James's accession. Several of their number went into Spain to stir up the Spanish court against the queen, and to request a foreign army for the subjugation of England. The death of Elizabeth took place while those proceedings were going forward on the Continent, and was the means of suspending the operations of the conspirators for a season. As soon as James's accession was known, the king of Spain endeavoured to enter into a negociation for peace, so that the conspirators were not at this time openly favoured by that monarch. It was supposed that some concessions might be obtained from James in favour of his Roman Catholic subjects: but in a very short space the leaders of the conspiracy discovered, that they were not likely to gain much by negociation. Unquestionably the Romanist party in England endeavoured to induce the King of Spain to attempt an invasion of the country: and it is equally certain, that their solicitations would have been taken into serious consideration if Queen Elizabeth had not died. Had the project of invasion been realised, the conspirators would not have proceeded to execute the Gunpowder Plot.

On the accession of James, therefore, there was a calm: but it was deceptive: it was only the calm before the storm; and to the eye of the careful observer, it indicated any thing but prosperity and tranquillity. It was evident to most men of reflection, that the storm was gathering: nay, there were indications of its approach, though no one knew how or where it would burst forth. The rolling of the thunder was, as it were, heard in the distance, though whether it would approach nearer or pass away altogether, was a question which no one could determine.

I have glanced at the various treasons with which the whole reign of Elizabeth was so pregnant: and the principles from which they flowed have also been slightly alluded to, namely, the principles of the church of Rome respecting the punishment of heresy, and the keeping faith with heretics. The doctrine of the church of Rome on this subject, as expounded by the Jesuits, and especially by Parsons, who at this period was one of the prime movers of every conspiracy against the English sovereign, was this, namely, that if any prince should turn aside from the church of Rome, he would forfeit his royal power; and that this result would follow from the law itself, both human and divine, even before any sentence was passed upon him by the supreme pastor or judge. This doctrine was a consequence of the papal supremacy. The doctrine of the supremacy is this—that the bishops of Rome, as successors of St. Peter, have authority, derived to them from Christ himself, over all churches, and kingdoms, and princes; that, in consequence of this power, they may depose kings and absolve their subjects from their allegiance, bestowing the kingdom of the offender on another; that excommunicated princes are not to be obeyed; and that, to rise in arms against them, or to put them to death, is not only lawful, but meritorious. Acting on these principles, Clement VIII. issued certain bulls, in which he called upon all members of the church of Rome to use their exertions for the purpose of preventing the accession of James, whenever Queen Elizabeth should depart this life.

Under such circumstances was James I. called to the throne. The papal party were resolved on the execution of their designs: and the pope and the king of Spain were so far implicated, that they were fully aware, if not of the particular nature of the intended plot, yet that certain schemes would be resorted to for the accomplishment of the grand object, which was the subjugation of England to the papal yoke. Had the conspirators been successful, they would have been furnished with all necessary supplies for their purpose by the court of Rome, and those states which were in alliance with the holy see. Such a combination could not have been defeated by human means, especially as the plot was carried on with the utmost secresy: but the watchful eye of divine providence was fixed on the country, and the designs of its enemies, as will be shown in this narrative, were mercifully frustrated. The bulls above alluded to were to be kept secret as long as the queen survived. They were addressed to the clergy, the nobility, and the commons, who were exhorted not to receive any sovereign whose accession would not be agreeable to the pope. The reasons assigned by his holiness for recommending such a course, were the honour of God, the restoration of the true religion, and the salvation of immortal souls. The Cardinal D'Ossat, to whom they were at first entrusted, wrote to King James on the subject, expressing a hope that he would openly profess the religion of his mother. It will be seen, in a subsequent chapter, that these bulls were committed to Garnet, who confessed that they had been in his possession, and by whom they were destroyed when it was found to be impossible to prevent James from succeeding to the English throne.

Never, perhaps, in the history of the world was a sovereign delivered from more conspiracies than Queen Elizabeth. The efforts of her enemies were unceasingly directed to one object, and that object was the queen's death. Not only were private individuals instigated to attempt her destruction, but the most extensive confederacies were entered into by almost all the papal sovereigns of Europe.

A remarkable circumstance is related of the hopes and intentions of the Spaniards, in the event of success in the *Armada*. A Spanish officer, who was taken prisoner, was examined before the privy council. He confessed that their object in coming was to subjugate the nation to the yoke of Spain, and the church to that of the pope. He was asked by some of the lords what they intended to do with the *Catholics*, as some must necessarily have fallen: to which question he promptly replied, that they meant to send them directly to *heaven*, even as they should have sent the *heretics* to *hell*. This statement rests on the authority of the chaplain to the army. It was revealed to him in order that he might publish it the next day, in his sermon, to the troops. He states, that by commandment of the council he did publish it to the army. In those days, there were no *newspapers*: nor was it then so easy to communicate intelligence by *placards* or *bills*. We find, therefore, that the pulpit was often made a vehicle for publishing the common news of the day. At a subsequent period, during the commotions between Charles I. and his Parliament, when the latter obtained possession of most of the pulpits, they were the only channels through which many of the people were made acquainted with the progress of the war. Whatever had occurred during the week was published to the people, from the pulpit, on the Sunday[6].

King James, therefore, succeeded to the English crown at a period when the pope and the papal sovereigns entertained the most sanguine hopes of re-establishing popery in this country, and when numbers of Jesuits and their disciples were ready to execute any treason which might be concocted.

---

[6] For a description of the proceedings of the Parliamentary divines in publishing the *news* of the day from the pulpits during the civil war, the reader is referred to my former work, *A History of the English Episcopacy from 1640 to 1660.*

CHAPTER II.

SKETCHES OF THE CONSPIRATORS.

The persons actually engaged in this atrocious deed were few in number: at the outset, indeed, very few: but the design was gradually revealed to others, though even when the discovery actually took place, the number was comparatively small. That there was a general belief among the Romanist body, that some great and effective blow would be struck, is a fact which I need not attempt to prove, since it is so well known, that no doubt can be entertained on the subject: but how the design was to be carried into effect was a secret to the great body of the Roman Catholics. The conspirators were thirteen in number. Their names were as follows:—

- Robert Catesby,
- Robert Winter,
- Thomas Percy,
- Thomas Winter,
- John Wright,
- Christopher Wright,
- Everard Digby, Knt.,
- Ambrose Rookwood,
- Francis Tresham,
- John Grant,
- Robert Keys,
- Guy Fawkes,
- And Bates, the servant of Catesby.

Of this number, five only were engaged in the plot at its commencement, the rest being associated with them during its progress. Several of them took no active part in the mine; they were, however, in the secret, and furnished the money necessary to carry on the work. Three Jesuits, as will appear in the narrative, were also privy to the design, and counselled and encouraged the conspirators. They were Garnet, Gerrard, and Tesmond, *alias* Greenway. I shall endeavour to place before the reader such particulars as I have been able to collect respecting all these individuals, before I enter upon the narrative of the plot.

Robert Catesby.

Catesby was the contriver of the conspiracy[7]. He was a native of Leicestershire: a man of family and property, and of such persuasive eloquence, that he induced several of the conspirators to comply, who otherwise, in all probability, would not have been implicated in the treason. Some of them admitted, that it was not so much their conviction of the justice of the cause that led them to engage in the business, as the wily eloquence of Catesby. He was descended from the celebrated minister of Richard III. Little, however, is known of him beyond the part which he acted in the Gunpowder Treason. It is evident that he was a man of considerable abilities; but being a bigot to the principles of the church of Rome, he was a fit instrument for the execution of any plot, however horrible. Whether he was influenced by the Jesuits, or whether prompted to undertake the deed by his own feelings on the subject of popery, is a question of no easy solution, since, in consequence of his death, when the rest of his companions were taken, no confession was given to the world, which would probably have been the case, if he had been brought to trial with the other conspirators. He was the only layman with whom the Jesuit Garnet would confer on the subject of the plot.

Thomas Percy.

This gentleman was nearly allied to the earl of Northumberland, by whom he was elevated to the post of captain of the gentlemen pensioners. He appears to have been a man of great violence of temper; and his conduct proves him to have been a staunch bigot to popery. Catesby on some occasions found it necessary to restrain his violence, lest his indiscretion should mar the whole contrivance. On one occasion, he offered to rush into the presence-chamber, and kill the king. He was killed with Catesby, at Holbeach, shortly after the discovery of the treason.

Thomas Winter.

It appears that Winter had contemplated a departure from England altogether, when Catesby, who had entered upon the plot, requested him to quit the country, whither he had retired, till an opportunity should offer of going to the Continent, and to come with all speed to

---

[7] In his youth he was entirely devoted to dissipation; but in 1598, his zeal for the church of Rome was suddenly revived.

London. The scheme was proposed to Winter, who evinced no indisposition to enter into the plot: on the contrary, he appears to have complied, with the utmost readiness, with all Catesby's plans. Soon after this interview he went over to the Continent, to reveal the design to some influential papists, with a view to ascertaining their opinions on the subject. Winter appeared at his execution to be penitent; but no hesitation was manifested by him at the first; nor does he appear to have entertained any scruples during the progress of the conspiracy. In many respects, he appears to have been an amiable man: but such principles as are inculcated by the church of Rome, are calculated to quench all those feelings of kindliness, which naturally exist in the human heart. The breast of Thomas Winter was steeled by his principles against the kindlier emotions of our common nature. It is related of him, that he dreamt, not long before the discovery of the treason, "that he saw steeples and churches stand awry, and within those churches strange and unknown faces." When he was taken in Staffordshire, an explosion of gunpowder took place, and some of the conspirators were scorched, and otherwise injured; at this time, his dream was recalled to his remembrance, and he fancied that there was a resemblance between the faces of the persons he had seen in his dream, and those of his companions. The recollection of the dream appears to have made a strong impression on him at the period when he was taken into custody.

Robert Winter.

This gentleman was the brother of the preceding, by whom he was drawn into the conspiracy. Robert Winter was added to their number some time after the mine had been commenced. The circumstance caused some distress to Thomas Winter, who petitioned the court at his trial, that, as he had been the cause of his brother's ruin, his death might be considered as a sufficient atonement to the law for both. Winter was taken in Staffordshire, where he retreated after the discovery of the plot. For some time, he was concealed in a house, whose occupant was a Roman Catholic. The circumstance that led to his discovery was somewhat singular. The cook was surprised at the number of dishes, which were daily taken to his master's room; he therefore, to satisfy his curiosity, peeped through the keyhole, when he saw a person sitting with his master. He was alarmed, both on their account, and on his own; but his fears for his own safety being greater than his apprehensions for Winter and his master, he determined to make a discovery to one of his relations. This step was followed by their apprehension.

Guido, or Guy Fawkes.

Fawkes was a soldier of fortune, who for some years was engaged in the Spanish service. Little is known of his early life, except that he was a native of the county of York, and received his education in the city of York. The writer of the *Life of Bishop Morton* informs us that the bishop and Fawkes were schoolfellows together in that city. His subsequent history to the period of the treason, is but imperfectly known. He appears to have been a bold and daring adventurer, as well as a gloomy bigot to the worst principles of popery; and was, in consequence, deemed by Catesby to be a suitable instrument for his purpose. His proceedings in the mine, as well as on the Continent, will be noticed in the prosecution of the narrative.

John Wright.

John Wright was early engaged in the plot with Catesby. It was agreed between these two individuals, Catesby and Wright, that an oath should be administered to all who should engage in the conspiracy. The oath will be given in the narrative. John Wright was killed in the struggle with the sheriff, in Staffordshire, where most of the conspirators were taken subsequent to the discovery of the plot.

Christopher Wright.

This person was the brother of the preceding, by whom he was induced to enter into the conspiracy. He appears, however, to have entered into the business with as much zeal as any of the rest. He was the first to discover the apprehension of Fawkes, on the morning of the Fifth of November. His advice was, that each conspirator should betake himself to flight in a different direction from any of his companions. Had this advice been followed, several of them would probably have succeeded in making their escape to the Continent. The conspirators, however, adopted another course, which issued in their discomfiture in Staffordshire, where Christopher Wright was also killed.

Thomas Bates.

Bates was a servant, and the only one of the conspirators who did not move in the rank of a gentleman. When the plot was concocting, he was servant to Catesby, the leader in the treason. Catesby observed that his actions were particularly noticed by his servant. The circumstance led him to suspect, that Bates was in some measure acquainted with their designs, or at all events, that he suspected that they had some grand scheme in agitation. In the presence, therefore, of Thomas Winter, Catesby asked him what he thought the business was, which was then in contemplation. Bates replied, that he thought they were contriving some dangerous matter, though he knew not what the particulars were. He was again asked what he thought the business might be. He answered, that he thought they intended some dangerous matter near the Parliament House, because he had been sent to take a lodging near that place. Bates was then induced to take an oath of secresy; when the particulars were made known to him. It was then stated that he must receive the sacrament, as a pledge that he would not reveal the matter. With this view, he went to confession to *Tesmond* the *Jesuit*, telling him that he was to conceal a dangerous matter, which had been revealed to him by his master, and Thomas Winter, and which he feared was unlawful. He then disclosed the whole plot to the Jesuit, desiring his counsel in the business. Tesmond charged him to keep the matter strictly secret, adding, that he was engaged in a good cause, and that it was not sinful to conceal the plot. Bates then received absolution and the sacrament, in company with Catesby and Winter. Such were the means used to draw Bates into the conspiracy.

Francis Tresham.

Tresham was also engaged in the plot at an early period. He was not one of those with whom it originated; but it was revealed to him when the parties were in want of money, to enable them to carry on their scheme. He offered to contribute 2000*l*. towards the grand object. He died in the Tower before the trial of his companions.

Ambrose Rookwood.

Rookwood was a man of fortune, and, until he became implicated in this plot, of reputation. He was not one of the original contrivers of the treason, but was drawn into it by a strong affection for Catesby, who appears to have exercised over him a most extraordinary influence.

John Grant.

Grant was a resident at Coventry, and, like Tresham and Rookwood, did not labour in the mine, but was made acquainted with the scheme after it had been concocted. Grant seized upon several horses on the morning of the 6th of November, supposing that the explosion had taken place, with a view to the seizure of the Princess Elizabeth, then on a visit in the neighbourhood. He was taken with the other conspirators in Staffordshire.

Robert Keys.

Little is known of this individual: but according to his own account at his trial, his circumstances had always been desperate, as well as his character. Such a man was, therefore, ready for any enterprise, however criminal. Fuller relates the following circumstance, which I give in his own quaint language. "A few days before the fatal blow should be given, Keies being in Tickmarsh, in Northamptonshire, at his brother-in-law's house, Mr. Gilbert Pickering, a Protestant, he suddenly whipped out his sword, and in merriment made many offers therewith at the heads, necks, and sides, of several gentlemen and ladies then in his company: it was then taken for a mere frolic, and so passed accordingly: but afterward, when the treason was discovered, such as remembered his gestures, thought he practised what he intended to do when the plot should take effect: that is, to hack and hew, kill and destroy, all eminent persons of a different religion from himself."

Sir Everard Digby.

This gentleman was descended from an ancient family, resident in Rutlandshire. His education was entirely directed by priests of the church of Rome, his father dying when he was only eleven years of age. He was introduced to the court of Elizabeth at an early period of his life; and soon after the accession of King James was knighted by his majesty. Sir Everard was made acquainted with the plot during its progress, when the early and original conspirators found themselves in want of money. He promised to furnish 1500*l.* He was taken after the discovery and was executed in London.

Henry Garnet.

Three Jesuits, Garnet, Gerard, and Tesmond, were implicated in this conspiracy: the two latter escaped to Rome, Garnet alone was taken and executed. It is remarked by Fuller, "A treason without a *Jesuit*, or one of *Jesuited principles*, therein, is like a drie wall, without either lime or mortar; Gerard must be the cement, with the sacrament of secrecie to join them together: Garnet and Tesmond, (whelps of the same litter,) commended and encouraged the designe[8]." Garnet received his early education in Winchester school, when Bishop Bilson was warden. It is said that he was engaged in a conspiracy among the boys, whose design was to cut off the right hand of their master. At this time Garnet was at the head of the school. His conduct in other respects seems to have been so immoral, that he was advised not to offer himself as a candidate for a scholarship at New College. He quitted Winchester for Rome, where he enrolled himself in the society of the Jesuits. At length he was made the superior of his English brethren, in which character he returned into England, to promote a rebellion against Queen Elizabeth. Other particulars respecting his subsequent career will appear in the narrative.

Thus have I endeavoured to give a brief sketch of the actors in this dark transaction. In reading the pages of history, we feel a natural desire to know something of the persons, whose exploits are recorded. The particulars, which I have given in this chapter, are such as could not so well have been stated in the narrative. All other matters, however, relative to any of the preceding individuals will be woven with the history, on which I am now about to enter.

Other individuals were taken and executed for treason, in consequence of their joining in the conspiracy; but the parties mentioned in the preceding sketch were the only persons, who were actually implicated in the plot by any decided acts. It is pretty evident, too, that very few persons, besides those actually engaged, were fully acquainted with the particulars of the plot. It was the policy of the conspirators to reveal the precise nature of the design to as few as possible, feeling assured that the smaller the number of actual traitors the less was the risk of discovery. They were also aware, that all, or, at all events, most of the Roman Catholics would join them, when the design was carried into execution. The *Jesuits*, who were privy to the plot, intimated to the great body of the Romanists, that some great design was in agitation, without specifying particulars. The actual plot, therefore, was confined to a very few persons; but that a plot of some kind was going forward was believed by the great body of the Roman Catholic population throughout the country.

---

[8] Book x. 34.

CHAPTER III.

PROCEEDINGS OF THE CONSPIRATORS, TO THE LATTER END
OF OCTOBER, 1605.

Enough has been detailed in the first chapter to show, that it was the aim of the Romanists, throughout the reign of Elizabeth, to overturn the church, and to assassinate the queen. On James's accession the same measures were resorted to by the papal party, while the plots for the destruction of Protestantism were as frequent as ever. In tracing the origin of the powder plot it is necessary to look back to the close of the reign of Elizabeth. In December, 1601, Garnet, Catesby, and Tresham sent Thomas Winter into Spain, with a view to obtaining assistance from the Spanish monarch against England. It was always found in the projected invasions of England, that one of the chief difficulties was the transportation of horses. To obviate this difficulty, therefore, the Roman Catholics of England, or Winter in their name, engaged to provide 1500 or 2000 horses for the use of the Spanish troops on their landing on our shores. At this time one of the English Jesuits was resident in Madrid; and by this man Winter was introduced to one of the secretaries of state, by whom he was assured that the king was anxious to undertake any enterprise against England. The king of Spain further promised the sum of one hundred thousand crowns, to be devoted to this special service, and that he would effect a landing on the shores of England during the next spring. Winter returned home at the end of the year, and communicated his intelligence to Garnet, Catesby, and Tresham. The death of the queen took place soon after, when Christopher Wright was sent over into Spain by Garnet, for the purpose of conveying intelligence of the queen's death, and also for the furtherance of the negotiation, which had been already entered into during the previous year. Fawkes also arrived in Spain soon after Wright. He had been sent from Brussels by Sir William Stanley and Hugh Owen, two Englishmen, who had been concerned in most of the treasons against Elizabeth.

Some of the Jesuits were concerned in all the treasons to which I have already alluded; and the gunpowder treason was managed by the same party, the actors being either Jesuits, or the disciples of Jesuits. Jesuits were their directors, their confessors, and their governors. "I never yet knew a treason without a Romish priest," said Sir Edward Coke, at the trial of the conspirators; and on Garnet's trial he declares, "Since the Jesuits set foot in this land, there never passed four years without a most pestilent and pernicious treason, tending to the subversion of the whole state." Shortly before the death of Elizabeth, and while the negotiations just mentioned were going forward in Spain, the pope, Clement VIII., addressed to the English Romanists the bulls to which I have already referred in a former chapter; by which they were instructed to oppose any one who should claim the crown after Elizabeth's death, unless he would promise not merely to tolerate the Roman Catholic faith, but to promote it by all means in his power. These bulls were to be executed, "*Quandocunque contingeret miseram illam fœminam ex hac vitâ excedere*,"—whenever it should happen that that miserable woman should depart this life. On James's accession, therefore, many of the Romanists were tampered with by the Jesuits, and persuaded not to render obedience to his majesty, as being a heretic. They were told by the Jesuits that they ought even to submit to death rather than obey a heretic. King James was, however, quietly seated on the throne, notwithstanding the secret practices of the Jesuits, backed as they were by the king of Spain and the pope. As it was dangerous to keep the two bulls in his possession, Garnet committed them to the flames after James's accession. Now it is altogether manifest, that the treason originated in these bulls of Pope Clement VIII.; for the conspirators argued, when the lawfulness of the undertaking was discussed, that if it was lawful to prevent James from possessing the throne, it was equally so to remove him though he had taken possession. I see not how this argument can be overturned by the Romanists; or how they can clear the rulers of their church of that day of the guilt of that dark transaction.

The circumstances of the country, therefore, at the time of James's accession were very peculiar. The pope had issued his bulls to prevent any but a papist from succeeding Queen Elizabeth; the king of Spain had promised assistance to the English Romanists; and Garnet, with some other Jesuits, and Catesby and his companions, were resolved to execute the designs of his holiness. It was under such circumstances that the plot was contrived. The king of Spain, however, refused to contribute money or to send troops when he heard of James's accession, with whom he wished to enter into a peace, and to whom he sent commissioners for that purpose. The disappointment of their hopes in obtaining assistance from Spain, led the conspirators, Catesby, and his brethren, to devise some other means, by which their object might be obtained. Frequent meetings took place; and various plans were considered and then relinquished. At length it was determined to undermine the parliament house, and destroy the king by means of gunpowder. It appears that Thomas Winter had some misgivings, lest the church of Rome should suffer in the estimation of the public if the plot should be defeated. Catesby replied, that the nature of the disease required a very sharp remedy. Winter's scruples were removed, and he entered into the project with all his energies. Still Winter started difficulties, which Catesby was most expert at removing. He objected the difficulty of procuring a place, from which they might commence their labours for the mine; but Catesby encouraged him by proposing to make the attempt, and that, if it failed, they might desist from any thing of the kind afterwards.

It seems that Catesby conceived the plan during the spring, A.D. 1603. Thomas Winter states that he was requested to meet him in town; where, after receiving a second letter, he found him with John Wright. At this meeting they conversed on the necessity incumbent on them of doing something for the cause of their religion and country; for these men, forsooth, professed to be patriots. Winter expressed his readiness to hazard his life in the cause; and Catesby made known his project. Thomas Winter then went to the Continent to meet Fawkes, to whom he was to make known the fact, that a plot was in agitation. They met and returned to England the following spring, when they were joined by Catesby, Percy, and Wright. At one of these meetings Percy came into the room and said, "Shall we always, gentlemen, talk, and never do any thing?" Catesby took Percy aside for a few minutes. Percy proposed to kill the king; but Catesby said, "*No, Tom*, thou shalt not adventure thy life to so small a purpose." At this time the plan was partially concocted by Catesby, but was revealed only to Winter. Catesby and Winter agreed that an oath of secresy should be administered before the plot was fully disclosed to their companions; who, though they were all anxious to enter upon any project, however desperate, were not yet acquainted with the plan which had been devised by Catesby.

Though Winter and Fawkes had met on the Continent, and had travelled together to England, yet it does not appear that the latter was made at that time acquainted with the treason. He came to England with Winter, with a view to the contrivance of a plot, but with the particular scheme projected by Catesby he was not acquainted, until after his return from the Continent. He was a reckless character, and ready to join in any desperate enterprise. Fawkes, in his own confession, declares, that the matter was at first broken to him in a general way by Winter. The parties were now five in number, namely, Catesby, Fawkes, Percy, Thomas Winter, and John Wright. According to agreement they all met together in a room near St. Clement's church, in the Strand. Here they administered an oath of secresy to each other on a Primer. When the oath had been taken, they all went into the next room, in which was the Jesuit Gerard, from whom, after they had heard mass, they received the sacrament. Gerard was probably acquainted with all the particulars of the plot. He was aware of the designs and intentions of the conspirators; for he waited in the room for the express purpose of uniting them together into a common bond for treasonable purposes. As soon as these ceremonies had been passed through, Catesby and Winter unfolded to the rest the plan which had been devised; and observed that the oath had been taken, in order that the plot might be concealed. Fawkes and the rest fully approved of all that had been done, entering into the plot with the utmost alacrity. In the spring of 1604, therefore, the plot was concocted. The oath was couched in the following terms:—

"You shall swear by the blessed Trinity, and by the sacrament you now purpose to receive, never to disclose, directly nor indirectly, by word or circumstance, the matter that shall be proposed to you to keep secret, nor desist from the execution thereof until the rest shall give you leave."

The next point was to secure a house near the House of Lords, in which the mine might be commenced. Fortune, in this respect, appeared to favour them, for during Winter's absence on the Continent, Catesby had heard that a particular house adjoining the House of Lords might probably be secured. Inquiries were made on the subject, when it was discovered to be in the occupation of a person named Ferris, who rented it of one of the officers of the House of Lords, by whom some of the rooms were occasionally used for parliamentary business. Percy was despatched by Catesby on the business, and, after some difficulty, he succeeded in becoming tenant to Winyard, the officer, as Ferris had previously been. Fawkes assumed the character of Percy's servant, the keys of the house being committed to his keeping. The name under which he now went was Johnson. They also hired another house, in Lambeth, for the purpose of stowing away the gunpowder and the wood, previous to its being deposited in the mine. The house was one in which Catesby often lodged. Their object, in depositing their materials on that side of the river, was to avoid detection, for they were fearful lest, by constantly entering the house in Westminster, the suspicion of some of the inhabitants might be awakened. It was at this period that Keys was admitted into the secret, and to him was committed the charge of the house in Lambeth. During these proceedings the parliament was adjourned to the ensuing February, an event which afforded abundance of time for their project; and therefore they agreed to quit London for a season, intending to return sufficiently early for the completion of the work before the opening of the session. The conspirators departed in different directions, in order to avoid suspicion. It was about a month before the commencement of Michaelmas term that the parties quitted London. About the beginning of the term, Fawkes and Winter met Catesby. They all agreed that it was time to commence their operations. When the parties arrived in London, they were rather staggered by the discovery, that the Scottish lords were appointed to assemble in Percy's house, to discuss the question of the union of the two kingdoms. In consequence of this occupancy, they were not able to begin the mine until the 11th of December, 1604. Late at night they entered upon the work of darkness! The powder had already been procured from Flanders, and deposited in the house at Lambeth. Not only did they provide themselves with the necessary tools for excavation, but they took in with them a stock of provisions, consisting of biscuits and baked meats, so that they might not be under the necessity of sending out to the adjoining shops for provisions, and thereby excite suspicion.

Now it must be remembered, that these conspirators were quite unaccustomed to laborious employments: yet their mistaken zeal in the cause of popery, which they seem to have regarded as the truth, induced them to apply themselves to the task with unceasing energy. They continued at their labour from the 11th of December until Christmas eve, without any intermission. Nor did they appear in the streets until that day. At this time they had conducted the mine under an entry close to the wall of the parliament house, under-propping the earth, as they proceeded, with wood. Fawkes, as being the least known of the party, acted as sentinel to give the alarm in the event of danger. In his own confession, Fawkes acknowledges, "I stood as sentinel, to descrie any man that came near, whereof I gave them warning, and so they ceased until I gave notice again to proceed." The object in placing Fawkes as sentinel was this, namely, that they might cease from their labour as any one approached, lest the noise should be heard and a discovery ensue.

Winter, whose confession was very full and minute, informs us that, during the progress of the work, they held many conversations relative to the steps to be taken after the execution of the deed. They hoped that the king and the assembled lords would fall a sacrifice in the explosion: but then there were the prince of Wales and the duke of York, and how were they to be despatched? It was supposed that the prince might attend the king, and share in the same fate: and Percy, who all along had evinced great boldness, undertook to secure the duke. Percy held an office near the court, and was acquainted with several of those who were employed in the royal household. He, therefore, undertook to enter the chamber, after the blow was struck, and, having placed others at the doors, to secure the young prince. It was also determined that the king's daughter Elizabeth, who subsequently became queen of Bohemia, and from whom the house of Hanover is descended, she being the mother of the Princess Sophia, and grandmother of George I., should be secured by some of their party in the country. The princess was, at this time, with Lord Harrington, in the county of Warwick, not very distant from Catesby's house. It was arranged, therefore, that the Roman Catholics of that neighbourhood should assemble, under the pretence of a hunting-match upon Dunsmore Heath, and that the princess should be seized during the confusion that would be consequent on the discovery of the plot.

Money and horses were also necessary: and the conspirators, at this stage of their proceedings, did not neglect to make provision respecting both. These and other subjects were discussed in the intervals of relaxation from their laborious employment in the mine.

Another very important topic was also introduced during these secret conversations: it related to the lords whom they should endeavour to save from the general destruction. It was determined that they should prevent as many of the Roman Catholic lords as possible from attending the house on that occasion; but that the rest must necessarily perish with the great body of the peers.

It was also debated whether they should reveal the project to any foreign princes. A difficulty here stared them in the face, namely, that they could not enjoin secresy by a solemn oath, as they had done among themselves: nor were they certain that the continental princes would approve of their design. They had little hope from Spain, because the king was too slow in his preparations, and was ready to enter into negotiations with James: France was too near, and could not safely be trusted. Such were their views of France and Spain.

These discussions took place while they were engaged in the mine. At this period parliament was again adjourned until the *Fifth* of October; on which account the conspirators ceased from their operations, intending to commence their labours sufficiently early to enable them to bring the matter to a completion, previous to the period fixed for the opening of the session. Early in the ensuing spring, they removed the powder which had been stowed in the house at Lambeth, into Percy's residence. Their labours were now resumed with redoubled energy. The foundation wall of the House of Lords was nine feet thick, so that their progress was necessarily very slow. They were obliged to chisel out the stones and the mortar; the wall being exceedingly hard, they advanced only about a foot in a week. These labours were continued during a fortnight, when they deemed it necessary to admit some others into their secret, to share with them in their toils. It was at this period that Christopher Wright and Robert Winter were admitted into their party. The same process was adopted in the admission of these men as had been resorted to in the first instance: they were sworn to secresy, and the oath was confirmed by receiving the sacrament.

With this accession to their strength, they continued in the mine until Easter, at which time they had advanced about half way through the stone wall. While occupied in their work, they were one day suddenly alarmed by a noise, which seemed to proceed from no distant spot. The conspirators had provided themselves with weapons, intending, if they were discovered, to sell their lives as dearly as possible. These weapons were now grasped by the whole party; and Fawkes was sent out in order to discover the cause of the noise. He soon returned to his companions, whose fears were banished by his report. Fawkes discovered that the sound proceeded from a cellar, which had been used for coals, and which was under the House of Lords. The coals were now selling off, the person who had rented the cellar being about to quit; and the noise, which had alarmed them, was occasioned by the falling down and the removal of these coals. This cellar was most convenient for their purpose: for it was exactly under the throne. The grand object, therefore, was now to secure it. Fawkes soon ascertained that it was to be let. Percy immediately hired it, pretending that he wished to use it as a coal cellar for his adjoining house.

Thus far they appeared to prosper in their dark enterprise. The mine was now relinquished; and it was resolved to deposit the powder in the cellar. Their labours were discontinued; and all their energies were exerted in making arrangements to secure the success of their design[9].

Hitherto Catesby had himself borne the expenses of the treasonable undertaking; but his resources were insufficient for the charge of maintaining the party, for the rent of several houses, and for the purchase of the materials with which the scheme was to be carried into effect. It was deemed necessary, therefore, that some monied person or persons should be made acquainted with the design, in order that pecuniary aid might be procured: and Catesby proposed that he and Percy, and another of the conspirators, should be permitted to disclose their secret to such persons as they, in their discretion, might deem desirable. The proposition was agreed to by the whole party, who now amounted to seven in number. This plan was adopted, because the parties thought, that several of the wealthy Romanists would be willing

---

[9] "In piercing through the wall nine foot thick," says Fuller, "they erroneously conceived that they thereby hewed forth their own way to heaven. But they digged more with their *silver* in an hour, than with their *iron* in many daies; namely, when discovering a cellar hard by, they hired the same, and the pioneers saved much of their pains by the advantage thereof."—b. x. p. 35. They were led to believe, from this circumstance, that God was evidently favourable to their design.

to contribute pecuniary aid, though they might be unwilling to disclose their names to the whole number of the conspirators. Having made this arrangement, Fawkes was employed in depositing a large quantity of powder and wood in the cellar which had recently been taken. The house was cleared of all those things which might have awakened suspicion, while everything was placed in the cellar,—a place which no one visited.

They began now to contemplate making another trial of their friends on the Continent. Catesby proposed that Fawkes should go over, assigning two reasons for his absence; *first*, that he might not be seen in England for a time; and *secondly*, that he might acquaint Sir William Stanley and Mr. Owen with their proceedings. It was, however, determined that the same oath of secrecy should be administered to these two gentlemen.

Fawkes quitted England about Easter. Stanley was absent from Brussels, to which place Fawkes had repaired; but he made the matter known to Owen, who cordially entered into the project. In the month of August, Fawkes again returned to England.

About the same time, Catesby and Percy met in the city of Bath, for the purpose of calling in others to render pecuniary assistance agreeably to their previous determination. It was at this stage of the plot, that Sir Everard Digby and Francis Tresham were made acquainted with the design. Neither of these gentlemen scrupled to enter into the plot. It was a most extraordinary thing, that gentlemen, otherwise of strict integrity, should have been so influenced by their religious views, as to concur in such a design without hesitation, which seems to have been the case. Sir Everard Digby engaged to furnish 1500*l.*, and Mr. Tresham 2000*l.*, towards the accomplishment of the object. Percy also promised to obtain as large a sum as possible from the rents of the earl of Northumberland. Rookwood and Grant were made acquainted with the plot about the same time; so that the number of the conspirators was now completed. These gentlemen, however, never entered the mine: they were merely privy to the treason, and promoted it by rendering pecuniary assistance.

When these matters were arranged between Catesby, Percy, and Tresham, Fawkes and Thomas Winter procured some fresh powder, and placed it in the cellar, as they intended it should stand for the explosion. All things being thus arranged by the conspirators, the parliament was again prorogued until the *Fifth* of November; an event which dispersed the party for a time. This third prorogation alarmed the conspirators, who imagined that their plot was discovered. To ascertain whether their suspicions were well founded, they mingled with the crowd on the day of prorogation, in order that they might watch the proceedings of the commissioners. They were satisfied that their suspicions were groundless; so that they went into the country in high spirits. About ten days previous to the *Fifth* of November, Catesby and Fawkes returned to the neighbourhood of London. Several of the traitors met together at *White Webbs*, on *Enfield Chase*. At this time, they were informed, that the prince of Wales would not be present at the opening of parliament. Whereupon, they determined on seizing him after the explosion. The duke of York, afterwards Charles I., was so safely guarded, that they entertained but slight hopes of getting him into their power. Down to the end of October, therefore, all things seemed to favour the designs of the conspirators, while the intended victims were unconscious of the danger to which they were exposed. Still the watchful eye of Divine providence was fixed upon the king and the peers; and the schemes of the traitors, secretly as they were carried on, were revealed, by one of those remarkable events, which no human understanding can fathom. The remark of Fuller on the frequent prorogation of parliament deserves attention: "As if Divine providence had given warning to these traitors (by the slow proceedings, and oft adjourning of the parliament), mean time seriously to consider, what they went about, and seasonably to desist from so damnable a design, as suspicious at last it would be ruined, which so long had been retarded. But, no *taking off their wheels* will stay those *chariots* from drowning, which God hath decreed shall be swallowed in the *Red Sea*[10]."

I have now brought the narrative down to the latter end of October, 1605. The conspirators were in and near London, Fawkes alone, as the individual who was to fire the train, taking his post in the cellar, or the adjoining house, as Catesby's servant. The parties were very cautious in all their proceedings, so that they met together secretly, whenever a meeting was necessary. As the powder and the wood were deposited in the cellar, and nothing remained to be done in London, the conspirators hovered near, leaving Fawkes to manage the firing of the train. They were full of sanguine expectations respecting the event, and busied themselves at this period, in forming plans for securing the young princes, and for carrying their ulterior designs into execution. Their attempt was, however, frustrated by an overruling providence!

---

[10] Book x. 35.

CHAPTER IV.

THE JESUITS PRIVY TO THE PLOT. THE NARRATIVE CONTINUED DOWN TO THE PERIOD OF THE DISCOVERY OF THE TREASON.

Before the narrative is carried further, it will be desirable to allude to those clerical individuals who were privy to this conspiracy. The actors were, as has been seen, laymen; but there were some priests of the church of Rome, and members of the order of Jesuits, who were no less implicated in the design than those who actually worked in the mine. Garnet, Gerard, and Tesmond, were Englishmen by birth; and yet, for the sake of advancing the interests of the church of Rome, they hesitated not to enter into the plot. Garnet was evidently a man of considerable attainments; nor is there any reason to believe that he was not, in many respects, an amiable man. His principles however, were such, that he could without scruple enter into a conspiracy against his sovereign and his country. There is reason to believe that he was privy to the design from the commencement, if he did not even suggest it to Catesby. At all events these Jesuits were made acquainted with all the proceedings of the conspirators, whom they aided and encouraged in their work, by such counsel as the church of Rome is accustomed to impart to her deluded votaries.

Even Catesby at one time had his scruples. He was not satisfied that it was right to sacrifice several Roman Catholic peers, who would be present at the opening of the session. His scruples were submitted to Garnet. It is, however, more than probable, that Catesby applied to Garnet, in order that he might be able to remove the scruples of others, should any arise. A case, therefore, was proposed, and to the following effect: "Whether, for the good of the church against heretics, it would be lawful, amongst many nocents, to destroy some innocents?" Garnet replied, that, if the advantage to the church would be greater, by taking away some of the Roman Catholic lords, together with many of their enemies, it would be lawful to destroy them all. "Indeed," says Fuller, "the good husbandman in the Gospel, permitted the *tares* to grow for the corne's sake; whereas here, by the contrary counsel of the *Jesuit*, the corn (so they reputed it,) was to be rooted up for the tares' sake[11]." He gave also an illustration from the case of a besieged town, which must be subjected to the horrors of war, even though some friends of the besiegers are dwelling within its walls. It was this determination of

---

[11] Book x. 36.

Garnet's, that quieted the doubts of the whole party throughout the proceedings. Rookwood was staggered, when the matter was first proposed to him; but he was satisfied when Catesby mentioned Garnet's decision.

The Jesuit wished to obtain the formal consent of the pope; but Catesby argued that it had been already granted, in the two bulls, the object of which was to prevent James from succeeding to the throne. Keys was induced to enter into the plot by these arguments; while Bates, Catesby's servant, was assured by another Jesuit, not only that he might lawfully conceal, but actually participate in the treason.

It has been already stated, that Bates confessed to Tesmond. In the church of Rome, confession precedes the sacrament; and in confession, Bates revealed all the particulars of the plot; still he was encouraged in the treason by his ghostly counsellor. In short, the evidence of the participation of the Jesuits in the plot is of such a description, that it cannot be disputed by any one who examines it.

The narrative has already been brought down to the autumn of 1605, when the parliament was prorogued from October to November the 5th. On Saturday evening, October 26, ten days previous to the day fixed for the opening of parliament, a letter, addressed to Lord Monteagle, was delivered, by a person unknown, to his lordship's footman, in the street, with a strict injunction to deliver it into his master's own hands. This circumstance took place at seven o'clock, just as the nobleman was about to sit down to supper. The letter was put into his lordship's hand by the servant. On opening it, he found it written in a very illegible hand, and without date or subscription. Monteagle summoned one of his attendants, to assist him in deciphering the epistle, which was couched in the following terms:—

"My lord,

"Out of the love I bear to some of your friends, I have a care of your preservation; therefore, I would advise you, as you tender your life, to devise some excuse to shift off your attendance at this parliament; for God and man have concurred to punish the wickedness of this time. And think not slightly of this advertisement, but retire yourself into your country, where you may expect the event in safety. For though there be no appearance of any stir, *yet I say they shall receive a terrible blow this parliament, and yet they shall not see who hurts them.* This council is not to be contemned, because it may do you good, and can do you no harm; *for the danger is past, as soon as you have burnt the letter*: and I hope God will give you the grace to make a good use of it, to whose holy protection I commend you[12]."

Dark, indeed, were the words. In the first instance, Monteagle viewed the matter as a *hoax*, intended to prevent him from attending the opening of the session. Still he deemed it the safest course not to conceal its contents. Accordingly he hastened off to Whitehall at that late hour, when, too, the streets of London were not lighted as they are in our day, and submitted the letter to the earl of Salisbury, Cecil, one of the secretaries of state. It does not appear that Cecil laid much stress upon the letter; at the same time he expressed an opinion, that it might refer to some design of the papists, respecting which he had received some information from various quarters. His information, however, did not relate to any plot; but merely to an attempt, on the part of the Romanists, at the commencement of the session, to obtain a toleration for their worship, and the relaxation of some of the penal laws.

Various attempts have been made to shift the odium of the conspiracy from the church of Rome, and also from any members of that church. Some Roman Catholic writers have not scrupled to say, that the whole was a trick of Cecil's, and that King James was privy to the design, which was entered upon by the court, for the purpose of rendering the Romanists odious, and to pave the way for more stringent laws against recusants.

The assertion that the whole plot was a trick of Cecil's, intended to render the Romanists odious to their countrymen, was not advanced till sixty years after the event. No one at the time questioned the reality of the conspiracy. The confessions of the parties, and the secret letters of Sir Everard Digby, preclude the possibility of even entertaining such an absurd notion. Not one of the conspirators complained of being deceived into the plot, either at his trial or execution; nor did any of their apologists deny the fact of the treason. The assertion was worthy of that church from whom it proceeded. Mr. Hallam, a most unexceptionable witness, thus argues on this point: "But to deny that there was such a plot, or, which is the same thing, to throw the whole on the contrivance and management of Cecil, as has sometimes been done, argues great effrontery in those who lead, and great stupidity in those who follow. The letter to Monteagle, the discovery of the powder, the simultaneous rising in arms in Warwickshire,—are as indisputable as any facts in history. What, then, had Cecil to do with the plot, except

---

[12] "A strange letter, from a strange hand, by a strange messenger: without date to it, name at it, and (I had almost said) sense in it. A letter which, even when it was opened, was still sealed, such the affected obscurity therein."—Fuller. Book x. 26.

that he hit upon the clue to the dark allusions in the letter to Monteagle, of which he was courtier enough to let the king take the credit? James's admirers have always reckoned this, as he did himself, a vast proof of sagacity: yet there seems no great acuteness in the discovery, even if it had been his own. He might have recollected the circumstances of his father's catastrophe, which would naturally put him on the scent of gunpowder[13]."

In recent times, however, it has been the policy of Roman Catholic writers to represent the conspiracy as the act of a few desperate characters. Desperate, indeed, they were; yet they were not men of desperate fortunes; nor had they suffered under the execution of the laws; but the sole principle that influenced them was one of religion. They were willing to risk all for the sake of promoting the interests of the church of Rome. It will also be seen hereafter that the pope, and some papal sovereigns, approved of the deed.

As to the report that the court were aware of the design long before the search, which was made in consequence of the letter, it is as destitute of foundation as the other. The court knew that some design was on foot: nor were they surprised, since such had been the case throughout the reign of Elizabeth; and the court was still composed of the same great statesmen. As to any knowledge of this particular plot, the court were not in possession of it. The king of France had informed the ministers that some secret plot was going on; but beyond this information the court had no knowledge on the subject. The secular priests, also, who were protected by Bancroft, intimated that some dark plot was concocting; but they were as ignorant of the particulars as the ministers. All the information, which James and his ministers received from the Continent, amounted merely to an assurance that a treason was hatching; but respecting the traitors and their proceedings they could learn nothing. These intimations undoubtedly rendered Cecil and James suspicious of the letter to Monteagle; but the letter conveyed the first certain intelligence that the danger was so near and so imminent.

When Cecil had read the letter, he laid it before the lord chamberlain and the earls of Worcester and Northampton. Monteagle was anxious that it should receive every consideration. They immediately connected the letter with the intelligence respecting the designs of the papists, of which they had been previously warned. It was determined, therefore, to submit the letter to the king, and not to take any steps in the business until they had obtained his majesty's orders.

---

[13] Hallam's *Const. Hist.*, i. 555.

On Thursday, October 31st, the king returned from Royston; and the next day Cecil submitted the letter to his inspection. It appears that Cecil offered no opinion concerning the letter; he merely placed it in his majesty's hands. After a little pause, the king expressed an opinion that it ought not to be despised. Cecil, perceiving that the king viewed the matter more seriously than he had anticipated, referred him to one sentence, *"for the danger is past as soon as you have burnt the letter,"* which he conceived must have been written by a fool or a madman, since if the danger was past as soon as the letter was destroyed, as if burning the letter could ward off the danger, the warning was of small consequence. The king connected the expression with the former sentence, *"That they should receive a terrible blow at this parliament, and yet should not see who hurt them."* Taking the two sentences together, the king immediately fancied that there was an allusion to some attempt by gunpowder. An insurrection, or any other attempt, during the sitting of parliament, could not be unseen; could not be momentarily executed. The king interpreted the clause thus, that the danger would be sudden and as quickly over as the burning of the paper in the fire, taking the words *as soon* in the sense of *as quickly*. He suggested, therefore, that the letter must refer to an explosion of gunpowder, and that the spot chosen for it must be under or near the House of Lords.

It is remarkable that Cecil himself had intimated to some of his colleagues, before the king's return from Royston, that the letter must refer to an explosion of gunpowder: the very same suspicion also crossed the mind of the earl of Suffolk, the lord chamberlain. This suspicion, however, was concealed from the king by the two statesmen. His majesty instantly took the same view of the letter, though he was totally unacquainted with the opinions of his two councillors. Popish authors have laboured to prove, that the treason was either planned by, or at least known to, the court, because the king so readily referred the letter to an explosion by gunpowder. Cecil and Suffolk had conceived the same opinion, though it does not appear that they thought of gunpowder secreted under the House of Lords. But what proof does this circumstance furnish of any previous knowledge even, on the part of the court, much less of contrivance? Was it strange that they should thus interpret such a mysterious letter? Cecil and Suffolk were fully aware of the plots which had been devised against Elizabeth; they knew that on more than one occasion, the traitors had contemplated the death of the queen by means of gunpowder. With these facts fresh in their recollection, it was perfectly natural to interpret the letter to signify some attempt of the same kind. In short, no other interpretation could have reasonably been put upon it. That the king himself should have suspected some attempt by means of gunpowder was also to be expected. He was well aware of the practices of the church of Rome; and it is probable that, on this occasion, he recollected the fate of his father, King Henry, whose death was accomplished by an explosion of gunpowder. To King James, therefore, really belongs the honour of discovering the gunpowder treason; for, though Cecil and Suffolk had conceived the same idea, yet they do not appear to have entertained the notion of a mine under the House of Lords. Besides, the two lords did not communicate their suspicions to the king. The remarkable part of the business, therefore, is the fact, that the three individuals should have so readily struck upon the same idea. It must, however, be stated that the interpretation put by the king upon the clause relative to the burning of the letter was not the true one: for it is pretty clear, that the writer wished Monteagle to absent himself from the parliament, and to burn the letter to avoid suspicion of being privy to the plot. But, though we may admit, that the king's interpretation of the clause was not that, which the writer intended, yet we must acknowledge, that his majesty's suggestion was most providential, and sufficient to justify the strong language used in the Act of Parliament for the observance of the Fifth of November. Let it be remembered that timidity was one of James's infirmities; and fear is usually very quick-sighted.

At this first interview with the king, no plan was adopted for their further course. The king suggested a search; but Cecil did not give his sanction. It appears to have been his aim to delay the search a little longer; and, therefore, he quitted the royal presence with a jest. What his motives were for not complying with the king's suggestion, cannot be ascertained. In all probability he was anxious to consult his colleagues, or he may have thought that the king's apprehensions relative to the concealment of gunpowder under the House of Lords were groundless. He did not, however, think lightly of the matter, though he jested with his majesty; for he immediately laid the whole case before the lords, with whom he had previously consulted, telling them what the king had said and suggested. It was agreed that Cecil should wait on the king the next day. The next day, accordingly, being Saturday, he introduced the subject again to the notice of his majesty. At this interview the lord chancellor was also present. It was now determined, that the lord chamberlain, by virtue of his office, should examine all the parts contiguous to the House of Lords, and especially the lower offices, in order that he might judge, from the appearances, which might present themselves, whether there was a probability of any such danger. To prevent the circulation of idle rumours, as well as to allow the conspirators to carry their plans as near to completion as possible, the examination was deferred until the following Monday,

November 4th, being the day preceding that fixed for the opening of the session.

It has never been satisfactorily ascertained who was the writer of the letter; but it is remarkable that the circumstance was made known to the conspirators within a very brief space after its delivery to Lord Monteagle. That one of the party penned it there can be no doubt; for they had proceeded with so much secresy, that no other person had any idea of such a design. By the interposition of Providence one, who was anxious to save an individual nobleman from death, brought destruction not only upon himself, but also upon all his associates. Neither the writer nor the bearer of the letter was ever known. It is probable that the writer himself was the bearer, as it is unlikely that the man who could pen it, and who felt so much anxiety about the life of Lord Monteagle, would commit it to the custody of another.

On Sunday evening, October 27th, the day after the delivery of the letter, a person called on Thomas Winter, and related the circumstance. This person was the servant of Monteagle, who had been called in to assist in deciphering the letter. Winter communicated the intelligence to Catesby, and recommended instant flight; but the latter was determined to ascertain the exact amount of information which had been communicated to Monteagle, which he hoped to discover by watching the movements of the government agents near the Parliament House. Winter, therefore, remained at White Webbs with Catesby, while Fawkes was sent to London to watch the proceedings of the court. Fawkes left them on Wednesday morning, October 30th, and returned in the evening, with the gratifying intelligence, that he found every thing in the cellar just as he had left it. They now hoped that the letter was disregarded, and that the danger of discovery was over. On the Thursday, Winter returned to London; and on Friday, he met Catesby and Tresham at Barnet. Tresham, who was related to Monteagle's wife, was suspected of being the writer of the letter, and was questioned on the subject by Catesby. He denied, however, that he had any knowledge of the matter; and it appears from Winter's confession that his denial was believed by the other conspirators. On Saturday, November 2nd, in the evening, Tresham and Winter met again in Lincoln's Inn Fields. On this occasion, Tresham related several particulars of the interviews between the king and Cecil. How he became acquainted with these particulars does not appear. Both Catesby and Winter deemed it necessary now to think of flight; but the former would not take that step without seeing Percy, who was not yet come up from the country. On Percy's arrival on the Sunday, he recommended that they should remain, and await the issue.

All the conspirators were now in great perplexity. On Monday, Nov. 4, Catesby went into the country, and Percy to the seat of the earl of Northumberland. Fawkes remained to fire the train, as had been previously arranged. At this time, therefore, they were uncertain whether they were discovered, or whether the treason was still unknown.

On Monday afternoon, agreeably to the previous arrangement, the lord chamberlain, accompanied by Lord Monteagle, and Whinyard, keeper of the wardrobe, proceeded to examine the rooms under the House of Lords. They came at last, to the vault or cellar, which had been taken by Percy. Here they saw the coals and wood which had been deposited there by the conspirators, to conceal the barrels of gunpowder. The cellar was at the disposal of Whinyard: and it appears to have been his privilege to let it for his own profit. On being questioned by the lord chamberlain, Whinyard replied, that he had let the cellar to Thomas Percy, with the adjoining house, and that the wood and coals were the property of that gentleman. At this stage of the examination, the lord chamberlain saw a man standing in a corner of the cellar, who stated that he was Percy's servant, and that he was left by his master in charge of the house and cellar. This individual was Guy Fawkes, who was appointed to fire the train. The lord chamberlain carelessly remarked to Fawkes, that his master was well provided, by his large stock of fuel, against the blasts of winter. On leaving the cellar, Lord Monteagle intimated his suspicion that Percy was the writer of the letter. This suspicion entered his mind as soon as Percy's name was mentioned, recollecting the friendship that had subsisted between them [14].

---

[14] I quote the following passage from *The Continuation of the History of England from Sir James Mackintosh*, in *Lardner's Cabinet Cyclopædia*, for the purpose of showing how unqualified the continuator is for the task which he has undertaken: "Search was accordingly made, and the powder was found concealed under billets of wood, and fagots: but all was left in the same state as before, to lull the conspirators into security." Such is the way in which this gentleman writes history. It will be seen from the narrative, that at the search to which this writer refers, the gunpowder was not discovered. The parties returned to the council, and having made their report, it was debated whether the search should be carried further. What dependance can be placed on the statements of a writer who confounds two circumstances with each other, or rather is not aware, of more than one search, or attempt at a search having been made!

The lord chamberlain returned immediately to the king, to whom, with the council, he related all that he had seen, mentioning also the suspicion of Lord Monteagle respecting Percy. He expressed his surprise that so large a quantity of fuel should be deposited in the cellar, when it was well known, that the house was seldom occupied by Percy. It appears, too, that he did not consider that the appearance of Fawkes was much like that of a servant.

The king still insisted, that it was necessary to make a rigid search, and that the wood and coals must be removed. It occurred to him, that they were placed there to conceal the gunpowder, for it was his majesty's firm conviction, that some such attempt was alluded to by the writer of the letter. The members of the council who were then present, concurred also in the same opinion. Still, they were in doubt as to the mode in which the search should be conducted. They were, on the one hand, anxious for the safety of the king's person, and on the other, fearful lest, if nothing of the kind should be discovered, they might be exposed to ridicule for entertaining groundless fears, unbecoming in statesmen and the ministers of the crown. It was suggested, also, that if the search proved fruitless, the earl of Northumberland might feel himself aggrieved, in consequence of his relationship to Percy, the owner of the house. All the members of the council agreed in the necessity of instituting a search: but their opinions respecting the manner in which it should be effected, widely differed. James insisted, that they must necessarily adopt one of two courses; either search the cellar narrowly, or leave the matter altogether, and go to the House the next day, just as if no suspicion had ever existed.

It was therefore determined at length, that a search should be made; but to prevent any sinister report, supposing nothing was discovered, it was ordered that Whinyard, the keeper of the wardrobe, should search the cellar, under the pretence of having lost some of the hangings, which had been placed in his custody. The king also suggested that the search should be conducted under the direction of a magistrate. Accordingly, Sir Thomas Knivett, a magistrate for Westminster, proceeded with a small and chosen band, to the parliament house, at midnight; while the king and his councillors remained at Whitehall. At the entrance to the cellar, they discovered Fawkes standing with his cloak and boots on, as if about to take a journey. He had just made all his arrangements within, when the magistrate and his party approached. Knivett apprehended him immediately, and then the party proceeded to remove some of the wood and coals. They soon came to a barrel of gunpowder: and in a short space, the whole number, amounting to thirty-six, were discovered. The next step was to search the prisoner Fawkes. They found on his person matches, and all other things necessary for his purpose. A dark lanthorn was discovered in a corner of the cellar. Fawkes made great resistance, when the party attempted to search his person; but as soon as he was secured, he expressed his sorrow, that he had not been able to fire the train, which he asserted he would have done, if he had been within the cellar at the moment when he was taken, instead of being at the door.

Besides the lanthorn and the matches, there was found on the person of Fawkes, a *pocket watch*! At that time, such a thing was very uncommon. He had procured this watch in order that he might ascertain the exact hour for firing the train. Such little incidental notices serve to show the state of the arts and sciences at particular periods, with their subsequent progress, better than the most laboured treatises on the subject. At this time, we learn, that small watches for the pocket were very uncommon; for the fact, that such a watch was found on the person of Fawkes, is mentioned as a rare circumstance. What a contrast between that period and the present day! And yet, in many of the fine arts, the age of James I. and Charles I. vastly excelled our own. In the mechanical arts, however, it was greatly inferior.

Sir Thomas Knivett, having secured Fawkes, returned to Whitehall, about four o'clock on the morning of Tuesday, the Fifth of November, so that the discovery took place exactly twelve hours before the time, when the train would have been fired, if the parliament had assembled. The magistrate communicated everything to the lord chamberlain, who rushed without ceremony, into the king's chamber, exclaiming that all was discovered, that all was safe, and that the traitor was secured. All the members of the council, who were in London, were now summoned to attend. Within a short space, Fawkes was placed before them, in order that he might be examined respecting this unheard-of treason. The prisoner appeared before them undaunted. Neither the awful situation in which he stood, nor the numberless questions which were put to him by those who stood by, moved him in the least. He not only avowed his participation in the treason, but regretted that he had not been able to execute it. Alluding to the discovery, he remarked, that the devil, not God, was the author of that discovery. During the whole day, the council could extract nothing from him by their examinations. He took all the blame upon himself, refusing to name any of his accomplices, but acknowledging that he was induced to enter upon the treason, from religious motives alone. He denied that the king was his lawful sovereign, inasmuch as he was a heretic. At this time, he refused to disclose his true name, calling himself *John Johnson*, servant to *Thomas Percy*. In a few days, however, being in a prison, he made a full confession of his guilt. Thus was discovered, one of the darkest treasons with which our annals are stained. Divine Providence interposed, just at the moment when the conspirators believed that their expectations were about to be realized. The merit of the discovery must certainly be attributed to the king. For though it is clear that the letter evidently pointed to something of the sort; yet before the treason was discovered, most of those to whom it was submitted, were in much doubt as to its meaning. The king alone suggested, that the vaults under the House should be searched: and in such a case, who can deny, that the thought in the king's mind was suggested by a higher power? "Let King James," says Fuller, "by reading the letter, have the credit of discovering this plot to the world, and God the glory, for discovering it unto King James." Wilson's words are much to the same effect; "being discovered by a light from heaven, and a letter from one of the conspirators, when the fire was already in their hands, as well as raged in their hearts, to put to the train."

Half an hour before the time, when it was expected that the king would enter the house, Fawkes was to place a match in such a position, that after burning during that space, should fire the train. He was to set sail for Flanders, for the purpose of obtaining succours from foreign princes; and the rest of the conspirators were to manage matters at home. It is said that those Jesuits who were privy to the design, but who could not publicly appear, were appointed to meet on a certain spot, on Hampstead Hill, that they might behold the conflagration caused by the explosion. This spot is still designated *Traitors' Hill*.

There is, indeed, a story, which would lead to the belief, that Fawkes was to have been sacrificed by his brethren in crime. I give the story, as it is recorded in the histories of the period, without pledging myself to its truth. At Tickmarsh, in Northamptonshire, resided a Mr. Pickering, who had a horse remarkable for its speed; Keys, one of the conspirators, is said to have borrowed this horse, shortly before the period fixed for the opening of the session. Fawkes, after having fired the train, was to proceed to St. George's Fields, where he would find the horse in question, on which he was to make his escape. This was the impression on Fawkes's own mind. It was further arranged, that Mr. Pickering, who was a well known puritan, should that morning be murdered in his bed, and secretly conveyed away; and that Fawkes also should be murdered in St. George's Fields, and so mangled, as not to be recognized by any one. A report was then to be circulated, that the puritans had perpetrated the atrocious deed; and to give some colour to this report, the conspirators were to appeal to the fact, that Mr. Pickering, with his swift horse, was there ready to escape; but that some persons who saw him, in detestation of so horrible a deed, had killed him on the spot, and hewed his body to pieces. Thus the mangled body of Fawkes was to be taken for that of Mr. Pickering, it being supposed that no one would doubt the fact, from the circumstance of the horse being found near the spot. It is added, that Fawkes, when he was convinced that it was the intention of his companions to put him to death, confessed the whole plot, which he would not have done, but for this treachery on the part of his fellow-conspirators. Such is the story, but I cannot vouch for its truth[15].

The fact, that the vaults and cellars under the House of Lords were then let out to hire for such purposes, furnishes a singular view of the manners of the age when contrasted with those of our own times. It appears that the inferior officers of the House made the most of their privileges. At this stage of the discovery, the king and his ministers were ignorant of the mine, which had been carried along from Percy's residence, under the walls of the House of Lords. This was not known until some of the conspirators had made a discovery of all their proceedings. Great was the joy of the nation when it became known that such a treason had been brought to light, and great was their gratitude to that omniscient Being, by whose gracious interposition, the dark designs of the conspirators were frustrated.

---

[15] In a work published shortly after the discovery, I find it positively stated, that Tresham was the writer of the letter to Monteagle. This merely shows what was the general belief at the time. See *The Picture of a Papist*. 4to. p. 124. 1606.

CHAPTER V.

THE PROCEEDINGS OF THE CONSPIRATORS ON THE
DISCOVERY OF THE PLOT—THEIR CAPTURE AT
HOLBEACH—THE MEETING OF PARLIAMENT.

It will now be necessary to look back a little on the movements of
the other conspirators. Fawkes remained to fire the train and was
secured, as is detailed in the last chapter. On Tuesday morning,
November 5th, as early as five o'clock, one of the Wrights called on
Thomas Winter, assuring him that the whole plot was discovered.
Wright stated, that a nobleman had called on Lord Monteagle, bidding
him rise to accompany him to the earl of Northumberland's, where it
was probably expected that Percy would be found. This was only an
hour after the return of the searching party to Whitehall. Some of the
conspirators were on the watch in various parts of the town; and Wright
chanced to obtain the important information, which he communicated
to Winter. He heard the nobleman, who called up Lord Monteagle, say,
The matter is discovered. At Winter's request, Wright went back to
Essex gate to learn something further: in a short space he returned,
adding, *All is lost.* He found a man on horseback at Essex door, who
immediately rode at full gallop up Fleet Street. Winter was conscious
that they were seeking for Percy; and he requested Wright to make him
acquainted with all that had taken place, in order that he might effect
his escape. Winter then quitted his lodging, being determined to
ascertain the worst. He went first to the court gates, which were so
guarded that no one could enter: he proceeded onward towards the
parliament house, but was prevented from passing by the guard, which
was posted in King Street. As he came back he heard a person in the
street observe to another, that a treason was just discovered, in which
the king and the lords were to have been blown up by gunpowder.
Winter was now convinced that all was discovered, and therefore he
rode off into the country. The two Wrights appear to have quitted
London at the same time.

Catesby, the leader of the conspirators, had left London the
preceding evening, in order that he might be prepared to execute their
project relative to the Princess Elizabeth as soon as the blow should be
struck. Percy also had departed from London that morning as early as
four o'clock, probably from having received some information
respecting the discovery. They made the best of their way into
Warwickshire, where they had previously agreed to meet.

London was all in commotion as the day dawned: the streets were
thronged with spectators, all eagerly inquiring what had taken place

during the night. It was soon ascertained, that a conspiracy had been providentially discovered, and that one of the traitors was already in custody. The satisfaction of the people was great at the intelligence, that no danger now existed, and that the king and the parliament were safe.

Fawkes was kept strictly guarded; and in a few days made a confession of the principal circumstances of the conspiracy.

The conspirators who had quitted London, previous to the fifth of November, proceeded to the place of meeting in Warwickshire. On Wednesday morning Grant and certain others seized upon some horses, which had been placed under the care of a riding-master. These horses were to be used at the *hunting match* appointed by Digby. Their object was to assemble large numbers of people under the pretence of *hunting*, and then seize upon the Princess Elizabeth. Having the princess in their possession, they hoped to be able to succeed in effecting a complete change in the government of the country. Had the plot succeeded in London, most of the Papists would have joined them. On Wednesday evening the conspirators who resided in the country, as well as those who had quitted London before the discovery, met at Sir Everard Digby's according to their previous arrangement.

It was now known that the plot was discovered; for those who had left London on Tuesday morning brought with them the intelligence. The question now agitated related to their future movements; and it was determined to make an attempt at open rebellion. This attempt shows the desperate character of the men; for they could not reasonably indulge in the expectation of success. They accordingly mustered as many forces as they were able, intending to await the issue of an encounter with the civil power, and hoping, amid the confusion consequent upon the discovery of the treason, to induce many members of the church of Rome to join them. In one of the letters of Sir Everard Digby, referred to in a subsequent page, a clear and succinct account of their intended movements is given:—"If the design had taken place, there could have been no doubt of other success; for that night, before any other could have brought the news, we should have known it by Mr. Catesby, who should have proclaimed the heir apparent at Charing-cross as he came out of town: to which purpose there was a proclamation drawn: if the duke had not been in the House then, there was a certain way laid for the possessing him; but in regard of the assurance, they should have been there, therefore the greatest of our business stood in the possessing the Lady Elizabeth, who lying within eight miles of Dunchurch, we would have easily surprised before the knowledge of any doubt—this was the cause of my being there." They mustered to the number of eighty persons only. From Warwickshire they passed to the borders of Staffordshire. Sir Richard Verney, the high sheriff of Warwickshire, pursued them. As they rambled through the country, they seized upon such arms and ammunition as fell in their way. On Friday, the 8th of November, the conspirators reached the house of Stephen Littleton, at Holbeach, in Staffordshire. The sheriff of Worcestershire sent a trumpeter commanding them to surrender, thinking that they were merely guilty of an ordinary riot, for he had not yet heard of the conspiracy. In those days intelligence was not so rapidly communicated, from one part of the country to another, as in modern times. The discovery took place on Tuesday morning very early: and the assemblage at Littleton's house was on the Friday after; and yet the sheriff of Worcestershire had received no information respecting the discovery of the plot. The traitors, however, were not aware that the sheriff was ignorant of their proceedings in London: on the contrary, they imagined that he was sent after them by a special order from the court. They prepared, therefore, to defend themselves, being resolved to sell their lives as dearly as possible.

The sheriff promised to intercede with his majesty in their favour, on the condition of their surrendering themselves, being unacquainted with their treason. Several proclamations had been sent into the country after the conspirators, in which the necessity of preserving Percy alive was strongly urged. But in those days a hundred miles were not soon travelled over. It is stated by contemporary authorities that the roads were very bad at the time; while another reason assigned for the slow travelling of the messengers, who had carried the proclamations, is the shortness of the days. It appears that travelling by night at that time was never contemplated. Thus on the third day after the discovery of the treason—the day on which the conspirators met at Holbeach—the authorities in the counties, in which the traitors were assembled, had received no tidings even of the existence of a plot.

While they were occupied in making their preparations in the house, a spark of fire dropped on about two pounds of gunpowder, which had been laid on a plate near the chimney, for the purpose of being dried. One of the party chanced to throw a log of wood on the fire; this raised the sparks, one of which fell on the powder, causing an explosion, by which the roof of the house was blown off, and the persons of Catesby, Rookwood, and Grant blackened and scorched. It was remarkable that a bag of gunpowder, of considerable size, which was lying in the room at the time of the explosion, was blown into the court-yard without being ignited, or none of the conspirators could have survived, and thus the whole of the plot would have been for ever enveloped in mystery. Catesby, Rookwood, and Grant were partly disabled by the explosion, "so bearing in their bodies," says Fuller, "not στιγματα, *the marks of the Lord Jesus Christ*, but the print of their own impieties." As the house had caught fire it was deemed necessary to open the doors and attempt to escape; but when the bars of the outer gates were removed to permit the conspirators to rush forth, the sheriff's men rushed in, so that escape was impossible. The battle now raged in the court-yard of the house with great violence. Catesby and Percy placed themselves back to back, and fought, though the former had been partly disabled by the explosion, with desperate courage. One of the sheriff's men levelled his piece across a wall, taking deliberate aim at Catesby and Percy, both of whom fell by the same ball, the former dead on the spot, and the latter mortally wounded[16]. The two Wrights also were slain, during the encounter in the court of Littleton's house; Rookwood and one of the Winters were wounded; and the rest were taken prisoners.

As soon as possible after the struggle, the conspirators were lodged by the sheriff in the county gaol. In a short space they were removed to London: and during the journey, and especially as they approached the metropolis, the people came in vast crowds to obtain a sight of men, who had concocted and almost executed so desperate a treason. Every one wished to see the faces of men, whose names and whose deeds were now resounded from one end of the country to the other.

Tresham remained in London during the commotion consequent upon the discovery of the plot. He was taken in a short time and lodged in prison. Robert Winter evaded the search that was made for him during a short space, but at length was apprehended. Sir Everard Digby was also taken. The actual conspirators were thirteen in number; four were slain in the conflict at Holbeach; the rest were all taken soon after the discovery of the plot. Tresham confessed in prison his share in the transaction. He died before the day appointed for their trial. Eight of them were brought to trial early in the next year, as will be noticed in a subsequent chapter.

On the 9th of November the parliament assembled. The king addressed them on the occasion in a lengthened speech, in which he dwelt on the proceedings of the traitors, and on the policy of the measures which had been enacted against recusants. James took a sort of review of all the dangers to which he had been exposed, alluding especially to the Gowry conspiracy. The speech abounds in good sense,

---

[16] "Never," says Fuller, "were two bad men's deaths more generally lamented of all good men: only on this account, that they lived no longer to be forced to a further discovery of their secret associates."— Book x. 36.

and sensible and judicious remarks are scattered over all its parts. Alluding to the characters of the conspirators, he very wisely observes, that there was nothing to induce them to enter into this conspiracy, except a mistaken zeal for their religion. He tells the lords and commons, that as soon as the letter was shewn to him, he interpreted certain expressions, contrary to the ordinary laws of grammar, to refer to some explosion of gunpowder. Having heard the speech from the throne, the parliament was adjourned until the 21st of the ensuing January.

When the discovery of the plot was known on the Continent, several of the sovereigns sent to congratulate the king on his escape. In the case of some of these sovereigns, their congratulations were sincere; but in other cases the language of deceit must have been used. The king of Spain and the pope, were among the most forward to congratulate his majesty; and yet with great inconsistency they sheltered and protected some of those individuals who fled from their own country, and were privy to the conspiracy. Osborn assures us, however, that the pope could not refrain from laughing in the face of *Cardinal D'Ossat*, when he informed him, that the Spanish monarch had sent a special messenger to the English court for that express purpose. Indeed, all these congratulations were hollow and insincere; but they would have been exposed to censure as men and as sovereigns, if they had not so far acted the part of hypocrites as to pretend to rejoice at the escape of the English monarch.

That the pope and the king of Spain, and some other papal sovereigns, would have rejoiced at the success of the plot, can scarcely be doubted, since their subsequent actions, as will be noticed in another chapter, proved that they favoured those who were privy to the conspiracy. It can scarcely indeed be doubted that the Spanish sovereign, and his holiness, and perhaps some other sovereigns, were acquainted with the designs of the conspirators; at all events, if they were not aware of the particulars of the plot, they knew that some conspiracy was in agitation, which was intended to be executed during that winter. Many of the Romanists on the Continent knew that some great deed was to be attempted, though they did not know the particulars.

The parliament did not meet on the 5th of November; but the following entry stands on the journals of the House of Commons under that date:—"This last night the upper house of parliament was searched by Sir Thomas Knevett; and one *Johnson*, servant to Mr. Thomas Percye, was there apprehended, who had placed thirty-six barrels of gunpowder in the vault under the house, with a purpose to blow up the king and the whole company when they should there assemble.

Afterwards, divers other gentlemen were discovered to be of the plot[17]."

On the 21st of January, the two houses assembled according to the previous arrangement, when a committee was formed "to consider the laws already in force, that tend to the preservation of religion—what defects are in the execution of them, or what new laws may be thought needful[18]." The lord chancellor gave special directions to the clerk to notice the peers who should fail to attend in their places; for there was a suspicion that certain Roman Catholic lords were implicated in the treason. Some were in consequence imprisoned and fined. In the House of Commons the same subject was discussed the first day of the session. The minds of men indeed could dwell on nothing else; nor is it surprising that such was the case; for a most horrible plot had been discovered, and the traitors were already in prison awaiting the sentence of the law. At length a committee was appointed to decide upon some course to be taken against *jesuits, seminaries*, and other *papal agents.*

The conspirators were tried and convicted at common law, as will be related in the next chapter; but the parliament seemed anxious to award some new punishment, beyond that which was ordinarily inflicted on traitors, on such culprits, for the purpose of marking their sense of their crime. Accordingly a committee was appointed in the lords to consider what extraordinary punishments should be inflicted. While they were engaged in this business, it was reported to the house, that it was not convenient to delay longer the trial of the conspirators, and therefore the matter dropped. The commons were no less anxious on the subject than the lords. The question was debated at some length; but at last it was determined, that the conspirators should be left to the ordinary courts of justice. On the 25th of January, however, the commons framed and passed a bill, which was sent up to the lords, entitled, *"An Act for Appointing a Thanksgiving to Almighty God every year on the Fifth of November."* When the bill was carried to the lords, the messengers stated, "that the whole body of the commons having entered into consideration of the great blessing of God, in the happy preservation of his majesty and the state, from the late most dangerous treason intended to have been attempted by the instigation of *jesuits, seminaries*, and *Romish priests*, had framed and passed the said bill in their house, as the first fruits of their labours, in this session of parliament, which they did very earnestly recommend to their lordships." The lords read and passed the bill in three days, without

---

[17] *Parl. Hist.* v. 125.
[18] Ibid. v. 141.

even going into a committee. This act is, therefore, the *first* in the printed statutes of the session. Several bills were passed against recusants and as a protection to the Protestant religion. On the 27th of May the session was terminated[19].

It may be mentioned, that the ceremony of examining the vaults is performed at the commencement of every session. Whether indeed it has been continued since the destruction of the two houses by fire, I am unable to determine; but as the cellar must still remain, I should imagine that the ceremony is still repeated. At all events, such was the case prior to the fire. The cellar is still designated Guy Fawkes's Cellar.

---

[19] During this session an Act was passed, by which every one was obliged to take the oath of allegiance—"a very moderate test," says Hume, "since it decided no controverted points between the two religions, and only engaged the persons who took it to abjure the pope's power of dethroning kings." Mr. Hallam's testimony is equally conclusive: "We cannot wonder that a parliament so narrowly rescued from personal destruction, endeavoured to draw the cord still tighter round these dangerous enemies. The statute passed on this occasion is by no means more harsh than might be expected."—*Const. Hist.* i. 554-5.

CHAPTER VI.

TRIAL OF THE CONSPIRATORS.

The conspirators, who had been lodged in prison, were frequently examined respecting the plot in which they had been engaged. Fawkes, Thomas Winter, Tresham, and Sir Everard Digby, confessed that they were guilty of the treason charged against them; and several of the particulars, which I have detailed in the preceding chapters, were revealed in these confessions. Catesby and Percy were slain at Holbeach, or some other information respecting the origin of the plot might have been obtained. It is probable, too, that Percy might have been able to give some account of the mysterious letter. For though the conspirators did not suspect him as the writer, yet it is evident that such was the impression on the mind of Lord Monteagle. To this day the subject is involved in mystery. Several conjectures have been formed, but the matter has never been cleared up; and it is likely to continue to be involved in mystery, until that great day when all secrets shall be unravelled, and all difficulties removed.

Tresham, as before observed, died in prison, and was thus spared the ignominy of a public execution. The other conspirators, Robert Winter, Thomas Winter, Guy Fawkes, John Grant, Ambrose Rookwood, Robert Keys, and Thomas Bates, were arraigned and placed at the bar on the 27th of January, 1605-6. The names of Garnet, Tesmond, and Gerrard, all jesuits, were also specified in the indictment, though none of them were taken. Garnet was subsequently apprehended; but the other two jesuits evaded the pursuit of the officers of justice altogether. The jesuits are specially charged in the indictment with persuading the other conspirators to act, on the ground that the king was a heretic, and that all heretics were accursed and excommunicated; and that, consequently, it was lawful, nay even meritorious, to kill the king, for the advancement of the see of Rome. The seven individuals before mentioned are then charged with consenting, and with contriving the plot, in conjunction with the jesuits. It appears to have been arranged by the conspirators, not to mention at first anything concerning a change of religion in the event of the success of the plot: and further, it was agreed not to avow the treason, until they should have acquired sufficient power to secure the completion of their plans. When the usual questions were asked they all pleaded Not Guilty.

The indictment was opened by Sir Edward Philips, one of the king's sergeants-at-law. This gentleman stated the case to the jury in a speech partly political and partly theological. Treason was the subject, but, said he, "of such horror, and monstrous nature, that before now, the tongue of man never delivered, the ear of man never heard, the heart of man never conceited, nor the malice of hellish or earthly devil ever practised." In the course of his speech he further stated, that the object of the traitors was "to deprive the king of his crown; to murder the king, the queen, and the prince; to stir up rebellion and sedition in the kingdom; to bring a miserable destruction upon the subjects; to change, alter, and subvert the religion here established; to ruinate the state of the commonwealth, and to bring in strangers to invade it." That such were their objects there can be no doubt.

Sir Edward Coke, the attorney-general, followed in a long speech, in which he stated, and then animadverted on, all their proceedings, from the commencement of the plot until its discovery. "Surely," said Sir Edward, "of these things we may truly say, *Nunquam ante dies nostros talia acciderunt*, neither hath the eye of man seen, nor the ear of man heard, the like things to these."

The particulars recorded in the preceding chapters were many of them taken from the confessions of some of the conspirators; and the speech of the attorney-general was founded, in a great measure, on the same confessions. Many things, indeed, could not have been made known in any other way. Several days had been occupied in examining the parties in prison; so that the law officers of the crown came to the trial amply prepared with materials. In tracing the progress of the treason, Sir Edward remarked, "It had three roots, all planted and watered by jesuits and English Roman Catholics: the first root in *England*, in *December* and *March*; the second in *Flanders*, in *June*; the third in *Spain*, in *July*. In England it had two branches; one in *December* was twelve months before the death of the late queen of blessed memory; another in *March*, wherein she died." He then specifies some of the acts in which Garnet and others were concerned, previous to the accession of James, and which have already been detailed in a preceding chapter.

Some important particulars are stated in the speech of Sir Edward Coke, respecting the conduct of the government towards the papists, after James's accession. During the reign of Elizabeth, severe measures were never adopted against *recusants*, as Roman Catholics were then usually designated in acts of parliament, until their own conduct, or at all events, the conduct of some members of the church of Rome, rendered it absolutely necessary. The laws, respecting which so much has been said by Roman Catholic writers, were enacted in self-defence. Had there been no treasons no such laws would have been devised; but when the members of the church of Rome planned, and endeavoured to execute, treasons, and of such a nature that the existing laws did not meet them, it became necessary to devise such methods as should not permit the traitors to escape. The origin, therefore, of the penal laws against the Romanists, in the reign of Queen Elizabeth, is to be found in their own treasonable practices; and the same remark will apply also to the reign of King James. Indeed, James was disposed to act with all possible leniency. Cruelty was foreign to his nature. Had the Romanists remained quiet, none would have been punished during his reign for their religious principles. Nay, so leniently did James act, even after the discovery of the gunpowder treason, that the puritans hesitated not to charge him with leaning towards popery.

The question relative to the penal laws is clearly and forcibly stated by Sir Edward Coke: "Concerning those laws, which they so calumniate as unjust, it shall in a few words plainly appear, that they were of the greatest, both of moderation and equity, that ever were any: for from the year I Eliz. unto XI. all papists came to our church and service without scruple. I myself have seen *Cornewallis, Beddingfield,* and others at church. So that then, for the space of ten years, they made no conscience nor doubt to communicate with us in prayer; but when once the bull of Pope *Pius Quintus* was come and published, wherein the queen was accursed and deposed, and her subjects discharged of their obedience and oath, yea, cursed if they did obey her: then did they all forthwith refrain from church, then would they have no more society with us in prayer. So that recusancy in them is not for religion, but in an acknowledgment of the pope's power, and a plain manifestation what their judgment is concerning the right of the prince in respect of regal power and place." This is the true state of the case respecting the laws against recusants. Sir Edward Coke specifies various treasons during the queen's reign, and then adds: "*Anno* XXIII. *Eliz.* after so many years sufferance, there were laws made against recusants and seditious books." He then alludes to the coming over of the *seminary priests,* who were Englishmen, educated and ordained on the Continent, and who came over into this country for the express purpose of stirring up rebellion, and to bring over the queen's subjects to the see of Rome. "Then," says he, "XXVII. *Eliz.* a law was made, that it should be treason for any, (not to be a priest and an Englishman, born the queen's natural subject,) but for any being so born her subject, and made a Romish priest, to come into her dominions, to infect any her loyal subjects with their treasonable practices; yet so, that it concerned only such as were made priests sithence her majesty came to the crown, and not before."

"Concerning the execution of these laws," he adds, "it is to be observed likewise, that whereas in the quinquencey of Queen Mary, there were cruelly put to death about three hundred persons for religion:

in all her majesty's time, by the space of forty-four years and upwards, there were for treasonable practices executed in all not *thirty priests*, nor above five receivers and harbourers of them; *and for religion not any one*." He proceeds: "Now, against the usurped power of the see of *Rome*, we have of former times about *thirteen* several acts of parliament, so that the crown and king of *England* is no ways to be drawn under the government of any foreign power whatsoever." This is an important point. It was no new thing in England to enact laws against the papal jurisdiction. The words of King James himself are very strong: "I do constantly maintain, that no man, either in my time, or in the late queen's, ever died here for his conscience. For let him be never so devout a papist, nay, though he profess the same never so constantly, his life is in no danger by the law, if he break not out into some outward act expressly against the words of the law, or plot not some unlawful or dangerous practice or attempt; priests and popish churchmen only excepted, that receive orders beyond the seas; who for the manifold treasonable practices that they have kindled and plotted in this country, are discharged to come home again under pain of treason, after their receiving of the said orders abroad; and yet without some other guilt in them than bare homecoming, have none of them been ever put to death[20]." The laws regarded not their religious opinions, but their practices. Will any papist assert that the priests and others did not endeavour to compass the death of Elizabeth, and to exclude King James from the throne?

It is remarked by Sir Edward Coke, in the address to the jury, that during the year and four months since James's accession, no penalty had been inflicted on any recusant. The conspirators could not, therefore, allege that they were driven to such a desperate course, by the harsh treatment which they had received. The plea of religion was, however, urged by these men: and that plea was especially grounded on the laws which had been enacted in the late reign against recusants. They appeared to exult in the fact, that the place in which the unjust laws, as they termed them, had been framed, would be the scene of vengeance.

When the attorney-general had finished his address to the jury, the confessions of the conspirators were read, and acknowledged by the parties. It was proved on the trial that Hammond, a jesuit, after the discovery of the treason, actually gave the conspirators absolution on Thursday, November the 7th. This act is conclusive as to the part taken by the jesuits in the plot.

---

[20] King James's Works, fol. 336.

A verdict of *guilty* was returned against the whole number who were arraigned at the bar. They were asked in the usual form why sentence of death should not be pronounced. Thomas Winter merely desired that his brother might be spared, because he was implicated in the treason by his persuasion. Fawkes objected to certain parts of the indictment, of which he said he was ignorant; when he was told that they were inserted as a matter of form. Bates supplicated for mercy, and did not deny his guilt. Robert Winter pursued the same course. Grant, after remaining silent some time, confessed that he was guilty of a conspiracy intended, but never executed. Rookwood at first attempted to justify himself, but at last acknowledged his offence, admitting that he justly deserved to undergo the penalty of the law; still he supplicated for mercy on the ground that he was neither the author of the plot nor an actor in it, but merely drawn into it by his affection for Catesby.

At this stage of the business a circumstance was mentioned to the court which had transpired in the prison. On Friday before the trial commenced Robert Winter and Fawkes were permitted to converse together in their cells. The former said that he and Catesby had sons, and that boys would be men, and he hoped that they would avenge the cause. They also expressed their sorrow that no one had set forth a defence or justification of the plot.

Sentence was not immediately pronounced; but Sir Everard Digby, who had been some time in custody, was arraigned at the bar on a separate indictment. He was charged with being privy to the plot,—with having taken the oath of secresy,—and also with open rebellion in the country with the rest of the conspirators, subsequent to the discovery. He had previously made a confession of his guilt, and, therefore, did not attempt to defend himself before the court. As he was preparing to address the court, he was informed that he must first plead either *guilty* or *not guilty*. He immediately confessed that he was guilty of the treason charged against him in the indictment. Sir Everard Digby evidently would not have been implicated in this conspiracy, but for his zeal in behalf of the church of Rome. So strong was his attachment to the papal creed, that he appears to have imagined that he should do God service by concurring with others in the destruction of heretics.

Having pleaded guilty to the charge of treason, he addressed the court respecting the motives that had induced him to enter upon such a course. He declared that neither ambition nor discontent induced him to unite with the other conspirators, but affection for Catesby the leader. He also confessed that he was influenced in his decision by religious considerations. Perceiving, as he said, that religion was in danger, he had resolved to hazard his property, and even his life, to preserve it, and to restore Romanism in this country. It appears that the Romanists were apprehensive of more severe laws being enacted under King James than those which had been carried by the late queen. There was no ground for such an apprehension, since King James was really anxious to treat his Roman Catholic subjects with great lenity. Sir Everard also requested that his wife and children might not suffer on his account. His last request was that he might be put to death by being beheaded, and not as an ordinary traitor.

The attorney-general replied to his address in a strain not unusual in that age, but which would not be adopted in the present day against the greatest criminal. Alluding to his very natural plea for his wife and children, Coke reminded him, in an insulting and sneering tone, of his attempt to kill the king and queen with the nobility of the country, asking where his piety and affection were when this scheme was devised?

When Coke charged him with justifying the fact he denied the charge, confessing that he deserved to suffer, but that he was a petitioner for his majesty's mercy. The attorney-general replied, that, having abandoned every principle of religion and honour, he could not expect to receive any favour from his majesty.

The earl of Northampton also addressed the prisoner, and in a strain somewhat milder than Coke. It would shock the feelings of the present age were the judge on the bench to revile the criminal at the bar, however notorious his guilt; but at that time such a practice was common. The earl of Northampton told him, that he had only himself and his evil councillors to thank. He also reminded him of his favour with Queen Elizabeth; and that King James was not ill disposed either towards him or the members of his church generally.

Judgment was now demanded by the king's sergeant on the seven prisoners mentioned in the first indictment, on the verdict of the jury; and on Sir Everard Digby, on his own confession.

The lord chief-justice proceeded to pronounce judgment. He first took a review of the laws which had been enacted in the reign of Elizabeth against recusants, priests, and the receivers of priests, specifying the causes which gave rise to those enactments, and demonstrating that they were necessary, mild, equal, moderate, and capable of being justified to the whole world. Sentence was then pronounced in the usual form.

Sir Everard Digby bowing to the lords who were seated on the bench, said, "If I may but hear any of your lordships say you forgive me, I shall go more cheerfully to the gallows." The lords instantly replied, "God forgive you, and we do."

On Thursday, January 30, 1605-6, Sir Everard Digby, Robert Winter, John Grant, and Thomas Bates, were executed at the west end of St. Paul's church; and on Friday, January 31st, the sentence of the law was carried into effect on Thomas Winter, Ambrose Rookwood, Robert Keys, and Guy Fawkes, in Old Palace-yard, Westminster, and at no great distance from the House of Lords, the scene of their recent treason.

Most of these wretched men evinced much penitence, both in prison and on the scaffold. It is remarkable that Fawkes, the most desperate of the whole number, appeared to be the most penitent at the time of his execution. They all declared their adherence to the church of Rome, dying, as they had lived, in her communion. They requested that the officers in attendance would communicate this their dying declaration to the world.

After the execution, their bodies, being quartered, were hung up in various parts of the city, as was the custom at that time with those who were put to death for treason. The heads of Catesby and Percy were fixed upon the House of Lords, where they remained some years after, when Osborne wrote his *Memoirs of King James*; unless, as he intimates, they had been removed, and others substituted in their room. It was reported when he wrote, that the heads then fixed on the House of Lords were not those of the two conspirators, but the heads of two other individuals procured, probably, from some church-yard, by the friends of Catesby and Percy, and fixed upon the poles for the purpose of preventing the discovery of the theft[21].

James acted with great lenity towards the families of the conspirators. By the statute respecting treason the property of the convicted traitor is forfeited to the crown; but in the cases of these individuals the children or heirs of those who were in possession of property were permitted to enjoy it. There was nothing vindictive in James's character; and he would have spared even these conspirators, if it had been possible.

Such was the fate of men who appear to have been guiltless of any other crime, and who would not have been implicated in this horrible treason, but for the influence of those principles which the church of Rome instilled into the minds of her deluded followers.

---

[21] Osborne's *Works*, p. 434.

CHAPTER VII.

THE TRIAL AND EXECUTION OF GARNET, THE JESUIT—THE ALLEGED MIRACLE OF THE STRAW—IS DECLARED A MARTYR.

Some time elapsed before Garnet was taken. He concealed himself in various places during the few months immediately subsequent to the discovery of the plot; the strictest search, however, was made; rewards were offered for his apprehension; and at last he was taken with Hall, another jesuit, and his own servant, in the house of a Roman Catholic. The servant became his own executioner in the prison. The proclamation against Garnet and the other jesuits, is dated January 14, 1605-6; but he was not taken at the end of the month when the other conspirators were executed. He did not, however, long elude the pursuit which was instituted.

On Friday, March 26, 1605-6, he was brought to trial at the Guildhall, in the city of London, before the lord mayor, several members of the king's council, and certain of the judges. During his imprisonment he was treated with much leniency, as he himself confessed on his trial. In the indictment the various names of the prisoners were specified; from which document we gather that he was known under different designations according to circumstances. Wally, Darcy, Roberts, Farmer, Philips, were the names assumed by Garnet on different occasions for the purpose of concealment. The indictment charged the prisoner, with concurring with Catesby, and the other conspirators, in the plot against the king and the state. The jury were sworn, and the prisoner pleaded *not guilty*.

Sir Edward Coke, the attorney-general, proceeded to open the case: and as this trial reflects much light on the whole conspiracy, I shall notice all those parts which appear to me of the most importance.

The attorney-general stated in the outset, that this trial was but a latter act of that dismal tragedy, commonly called the Powder Treason, for which several had already suffered the extreme penalty of the law. Throughout the trial he treated Garnet with great respect. From Sir Edward Coke's speech we learn, that Garnet was examined for the first time February 13th, and that from that day to the 26th of March, when the last examination took place, he was examined before the council more than twenty times.

In speaking of the treason, Sir Edward remarks, "I will call it the jesuits' treason, as belonging to them, both *ex congruo et condigno*: they were the proprietaries, plotters, and procurers of it." He then enters on a description of some of the treasons, which were planned in the reign of Queen Elizabeth, in which also Garnet was concerned, as I have noticed in a preceding chapter. Garnet confessed several particulars respecting those transactions in which he had been engaged; and among other things he admitted that the Romanists in England, after the bull of excommunication had been issued against the queen, were permitted to render her obedience with certain cautions and limitations, namely, *Rebus sic stantibus,* and *Donec publica bullæ executio fieret posset.* So that while things continued in their present state, and till such time as the bull could be executed, the Romanists might obey the queen. This was confessed by Garnet himself.

It appears that Garnet came over into England in the year 1586, two years before the sailing of the *Spanish Armada.* As early as the reign of Edward the First, the bringing in of a bull from Rome against any of the king's subjects, without permission, was adjudged to be treason; so that Garnet was a traitor by the ancient laws of the land, for the bulls against King James were committed to the keeping of that individual. The attorney-general had declared, when speaking of Elizabeth, that four years had never passed without a treason: and he adds, when he speaks of King James, "and now sithence the coming of great King James, there have not passed, I will not say four years, but not four, nay not two months, without some treason." In these treasons Garnet and other jesuits were implicated. The bulls which had been sent to Garnet before the death of Elizabeth, and which were intended to prevent the English Romanists from receiving any but a popish sovereign, were burnt by him, as already mentioned, when he perceived that King James's accession could not be prevented. There would have been danger in preserving them, therefore they were committed to the flames. The prisoner admitted that he had destroyed them.

It was shown on the trial that Garnet was privy to the plot in various ways. Though Catesby was the only layman with whom he would converse on the subject, yet he did not hesitate to confer with his brother jesuits respecting all the particulars. Greenwell pretended to confess himself to Garnet his superior. Confession is appointed by the church of Rome to be performed by the penitent in a kneeling posture; but it seems that, on this occasion, the two parties walked together; and during this walk Garnet heard all the particulars of the treason—how it was to be executed—and what was to take place subsequently. It was proved also that he had proposed writing to the pope on the subject, and that he met Catesby and some other of the conspirators in Warwickshire. It will be seen that he prayed for the success of the great action; and it is also a certain fact, that all the English Romanists prayed for the success of the plot, whatever it might be, which they knew was in agitation, though they were not acquainted with its precise nature.

On the morning of November the 6th, when the plot had failed, Catesby and some of the other conspirators sent Bates to Garnet, who was then in Warwickshire, to entreat his assistance in stirring up the people to open rebellion. Greenwell was at this time with Garnet. Warwickshire was appointed to be the place of meeting after the plot; and on this account the jesuits assembled in that county.

I have mentioned that Garnet admitted that he was acquainted with the plot, though he pretended that it was revealed to him in confession, and that consequently he was not at liberty to reveal it, a point which I shall notice in a subsequent page. The means adopted to procure his confession were curious, and perhaps not strictly justifiable. A trap was set for the prisoner into which he readily fell.

For some time he would confess nothing. In those days it was customary to extort confessions from prisoners, by means of torture, a mode long since abolished in this country; but the king and his ministers did not wish to render themselve obnoxious to the Romanists by resorting to the rack. Instead, therefore, of using torture, they employed craft; and though Garnet was an adept in the art of dissimilation, yet he was outwitted on this occasion. An individual was appointed as the keeper of the prisoner, who, by pretending to deplore the condition of the Romanists in England, as well as by complaints against the king and his ministers, at length succeeded in inducing Garnet to believe that he was well affected to the church of Rome. Two letters were written by Garnet, and entrusted to this man, the one addressed to a lady, the other to a priest. In the former letter he mentioned what things he had already admitted in his examinations; but the second letter was the more important. The letter was written on a sheet of paper, and appeared to contain matters only of an ordinary kind, such as any one might read. He had, however, left a very broad margin, which circumstance excited suspicion in the breasts of the council. Nor were these suspicions without foundation; for on examining the letter, by holding it to the fire, it was found that he had written on the margin with the juice of a lemon, beseeching his friends to deny the truth of those things which he had already confessed. He also expressed his hope, that he should escape from the powder plot from want of proof; yet he had confessed to the lords of the council, that he was guilty. It appears, however, that he did not really expect to escape; for in this same letter he applies the words of Caiaphas, who used them when speaking of the Saviour, to himself, *Necesse est ut unus homo moriatur pro populo.*

This letter, written with his own hand, was shown to him at the trial. It is still in existence. Some years ago it was discovered by Mr. Lemon in the State Paper Office, where it is still preserved, not only as a proof of Garnet's guilt, but also as evidence, that the principles of the church of Rome are not misrepresented by Protestant writers.

The man who had taken the charge of these letters conveyed them immediately to the lords of the council. The object was to have some public confession of his guilt on his trial. They were apprehensive that he might deny even what he had privately stated to the lords, which was much less than what he had admitted in these letters. The trap which had been set for him by the sage counsellors of his majesty was not set in vain.

But other evidence was soon produced. The individual to whom the letters were entrusted gained his entire confidence. Garnet told him that he was very anxious to see Hall, another jesuit, known also by the name of Oldcorn, who was then confined in the same prison. The keeper promised to arrange a meeting between them. For this purpose they were so placed, that they could converse together, while he, to avoid suspicion, took a position so as to be seen by both. At the same time two other individuals were secreted in the prison sufficiently near to hear all that passed between the prisoners. They conversed freely respecting their previous confessions and examinations—the excuses and evasions which they had prepared, and many other matters connected with the plot. During the conversation Garnet remarked to Hall, "They will charge me with my prayer for the good success of the great action, in the beginning of the parliament, and with the verses which I added at the end of my prayer." He added, that in his defence he should state, that the success for which he prayed related to the severe laws, which he apprehended would, during the session, be enacted against the Romanists. The verses alluded to were as follows:—

Gentem auferte perfidam
Credentium de finibus,
Ut Christo laudes debitas,
Persolvamus alacriter.

The next day Garnet and Hall were examined separately, when they were charged with having held a private conference. Garnet denied the fact in the most decided terms. The parties who heard the conversation were then produced: nor could Garnet object anything against their statements.

Garnet said on his trial that he once thought of revealing the plot, but not the conspirators. Cecil asked who hindered him from making the discovery; to whom he replied, "You, yourself; for I knew you would have racked this poor body of mine to pieces, to make me confess." Fuller remarks on this assertion and in allusion to the interview with Hall, that "never any *rack* was used on Garnet, except a *witrack*, wherewith he was worsted, and this cunning archer outshot in his own bow. For being in prison with *Father Oldcorn alias Hall*, they were put into an *equivocating room* (as I may term it) which pretended nothing but privacy, yet had a reservation of some invisible persons within it, ear witnesses to all the passages betwixt them."

These confessions, denials, evasions, and palliations were defended by Garnet under the plea of lawful *equivocation*, a doctrine then at least taught very generally in the church of Rome. Under shelter of this plea the jesuits were prepared, not merely to conceal or to deny any fact, but also to aver what they knew to be false. It was urged, and in books too, that such a course might be adopted on the ground that the parties reserved in their own minds a secret and private sense. Thus any question might be eluded: and this practice was publicly defended in a treatise licensed by Garnet and Blackwall. Certain instances are given in the work as illustrations of the doctrine. The following is one of these cases. A man arrives at a certain place, and is examined on oath at the gate, whether he came from London, where the plague is supposed to be raging at the time. The man, knowing that the plague is not in London, or that he did no more than pass through that city, may swear that he did not come from London. It is argued, that such an answer would agree with their intention, who proposed the question simply with a view to ascertaining, whether their own city would be endangered by his entrance. Such was the doctrine of equivocation, under the plea of which Garnet sheltered himself when he denied many things which were proved against him, and which he had himself confessed. Even Sir Everard Digby resorted to this papal doctrine of equivocation, as will be seen from the following extracts from his letters discovered in 1675, and published by Bishop Barlow, in 1679:—"Yesterday I was before Mr. Attorney and my Lord Chief Justice, who asked me if I had taken the sacrament to keep secret the plot as others did. I said that I had not, because I would avoid the question of at whose hands it were."—"I have not as yet acknowledged the knowledge of any priest in particular, nor will not do to the hurt of any but myself, whatsoever betide me." Speaking of a particular priest, he says in another letter; "I have not been asked his name, which if I had, should have been such a one as I knew not of." Again; "If I be called to question for the priest, I purpose to name him Winscombe, unless I be advised otherwise." And, alluding to the same in a subsequent letter—"You forget to tell me whether Winscombe be a fit name. I like it, for I know none of it." In another letter—"As yet they have not got of me the affirming that I know any priest particularly, nor shall ever do to the hurt of any one but myself." It is evident that he deemed it lawful to deny anything calculated to bring reproach on his church; and that he did not scruple to give a false name on his examination. From the manner in which he speaks, there can be no doubt, that he believed he might lawfully equivocate. And from whom had he learned this monstrous doctrine? From the church and her authorized teachers!!

The earl of Salisbury alluded on the trial to his denial of the conversation with Hall, reminding him that he was not questioned as to the matter of their conferences, but simply as to the fact. Hall confessed the fact, and Garnet, though he had so strongly denied it, then admitted the whole. On being reminded of the matter by Cecil, he replied, that when a man is asked a question before a magistrate he is not bound to give an answer *quia nemo tenetur prodere seipsum*.

Tresham, who died in the Tower, accused Garnet of a previous treason in entering into a league with the king of Spain against England. Before his death he was permitted to see his wife, who was aware of his confession respecting Garnet. Under her influence he dictated to his servant, being too weak to use a pen himself, that he had not seen Garnet during the last sixteen years, and retracted his previous confession in which he admitted the contrary. Now it was proved, and acknowledged by Garnet, that they had met several times within the last two years. Garnet was asked to explain Tresham's conduct; and his reply was, "I think he meant to equivocate."

Tresham died within three hours after dictating this letter. Mrs. Vaux, however, confessed that she had seen Tresham with Garnet at her house three or four times since the accession of King James, and that they had dined together with her. Garnet also publicly acknowledged that he had seen Tresham. A second confession of Mrs Vaux's was also read in the court, in which she admits that she was with Garnet at Tresham's house in Northamptonshire not long since.

Garnet made a long defence at the bar; and on the question of equivocation he defended himself with much subtilty. He declared that the church of Rome condemned lying; but he justified equivocation, which, he said, was "to defend the use of certain propositions. For a man may be asked of one, who hath no authority to interrogate or examine, concerning something which belongeth not to his cognizance who asketh, as what a man thinketh, &c. So then no man may equivocate when he ought to tell the truth, otherwise he may." When he was reminded that he had denied that he had written to Tesmond *alias* Greenwell, or sent messages to him, he said he would not have denied his letters if he had known that the lords had seen them; but supposing that they had not been seen he did deny them, and that he might lawfully do so. This has been confirmed by the papers in the State Paper Office. There is amongst these papers an original letter, in Garnet's own hand, to Mrs. Vaux, in which he acknowledged that he was so pressed by the testimony of two witnesses who overheard the conversation between Hall and himself, that he was, at length, determined to confess all rather than stand the torture or trial by witnesses.

Garnet endeavoured to shelter himself from the guilt of the plot, under the plea, that the treason was revealed to him under the seal of confession. At first he endeavoured to deny that he was acquainted with any particulars; but being forced from this subterfuge, he admitted his knowledge, but contended that he was bound to conceal all that he knew. He acknowledged also that he had concealed the treason with Spain. "Only," says he, "I must needs confess, I did conceal it after the example of Christ, who commands us, when our brother offends to reprove him, for if he do amend we have gained him." With respect to the Powder Treason he acknowledged, that Greenwell came to him in great perplexity in consequence of what Catesby had intimated. He consented to hear it, provided the fact of his doing so should not be revealed to Catesby, or to any other person. Greenwell then revealed the whole plot. He confessed that he was greatly distressed on the subject, "and sometimes prayed to God that it should not take effect." On being questioned why he did not reveal the conspiracy he stated that, "he might not disclose it to any, because it was matter of secret confession, and would endanger the lives of divers men." Cecil said, "I pray you, Mr. Garnet, what encouraged Catesby that he might proceed, but your resolving him in the first proposition? What warranted Faukes, but Catesby's explication of Garnet's arguments? As appears infallibly by Winter's confession, and by Faukes, that they knew the point had been resolved to Mr. Catesby, by the best authority." It was evident, therefore, that he did not merely conceal the matter; but that he was an active instigator of the conspiracy.[22]

With respect to Garnet's knowledge of the conspiracy, it is perfectly clear that the matter was not merely revealed in confession, but that he was one of the actors therein. Nor was the plea of confession

---

[22] Mr. Hallam observes; "The Catholic writers maintain that he had no knowledge of the conspiracy, except by having heard it in confession. But this rests altogether on his word; and the prevarication of which he has been proved to be guilty (not to mention the damning circumstance that he was taken at Hendlip in concealment along with the other conspirators), makes it difficult for a candid man to acquit him of a thorough participation in their guilt."—*Const. Hist.* i. 554-5.

consistent with some of his own declarations during his examinations. He admitted, that the treason was mentioned to him in the way of consultation, as a thing not yet executed; and moreover Greenwell did not implicate himself; he merely told of others, and consequently the seal of confession would not have been broken, even if Garnet had revealed the whole to the government. He chose, however, on his trial, to adopt this line of defence, namely, that he was not at liberty to disclose anything which was revealed to him in sacramental confession. One of the lords asked him if a man should confess to-day, that he intended to kill the king to-morrow with a dagger, whether he must conceal the matter? Garnet replied that he must conceal it. Parsons, the jesuit, maintains the same opinion. Speaking of Garnet, he remarks, that nothing was proved, "but that the prisoner had received only a simple notice of that treason, by such a means as he could not utter and reveal again by the laws of Catholic doctrine, that is to say, in *confession*, and this but a very few days before the discovery, but yet never gave any consent, help, hearkening, approbation, or co-operation to the same; but contrariwise sought to dissuade, dehort, and hinder the designment by all the means he could. He, dying for the bare concealing of that, which, by God's, and the church's ecclesiastical laws, he could not disclose, and giving no consent or co-operation to the treason itself, should have been accounted rather a *martyr* than a *traitor*."—See an answer to Sir Edward Coke's *Reports*, 4to. 1606.

It is remarkable that in a treatise published A.D. 1600, on auricular confession, a case is put to this effect; namely, whether if a confederate discover, in confession, that he or his companions have secretly deposited gunpowder under a particular house, and that the *prince* will be destroyed unless it is removed, the priest ought to reveal it. The writer replies in the negative, and fortifies his opinion by the authority of a bull of Clement VIII., against violating the seal of confession. This treatise was published at *Louvain*. Bishop Kennet remarks on this treatise, in his Sermon, November 5th, 1715, that it appeared "as if the writer had already looked into the cellar and had surveyed the powder, and had heard the confessions of the conspirators."

The proceedings were at length brought to a close; and judgment was demanded against the prisoner. When the clerk of the crown asked what he had to say why judgment should not be given, Garnet replied that "he could say nothing, but referred himself to the mercy of the king and God Almighty." Judgment was pronounced in the usual form, that the prisoner should be hanged, drawn, and quartered.

On the third of May 1606, the prisoner was executed on a scaffold erected at the west end of St. Paul's church-yard. Overal, dean of St. Paul's, with the dean of Winchester, exhorted him to make a plain confession to the world of the offence of which he had been convicted. Garnet desired them not to trouble him, as he came prepared to die, and was resolved what he should do. The recorder asked if he had anything to say to the people before his death, reminding him that it was not the time to dissemble, and that his treasons were manifest to the world. Garnet evidently had no wish to address the crowd; and without refusing the permission, he alleged that his voice was weak, his strength exhausted, and that the people would be unable to hear him, except in the immediate vicinity of the scaffold. To those who stood near, however, he said that the intention was wicked, and the fact would have been cruel, and that he entirely abhorred it. He was reminded that he had confessed his own participation in the plot. It was also stated, that he had acknowledged, under his own hand, that Greenway had asked him who should be protector? and that he had replied that the matter was to be deferred until the blow was actually struck. He confessed that he had erred in not revealing all that he knew of the plot; but he refused to make any further declaration on the scaffold.

He kneeled down at the foot of the ladder; but so distracted was he during his prayer, that he constantly paused and looked about him, as if in expectation of a pardon. He now expressed his sorrow in dissembling with the lords, but justified himself by saying, that he was not aware that they were in possession of such proofs against him. Then exhorting all Romanists to abstain from treasonable practices, he was launched into eternity.

Garnet was viewed as a martyr by his church after his death. Yet he had confessed himself guilty. When asked by some of the lords on his examination, if he approved that the church of Rome should one day declare him a martyr, he cried, *Martyrem me, O qualem Martyrem.* The church of Rome could not declare him a martyr however, unless they could allege that a miracle had been wrought at his death, or subsequent to it. A miracle therefore was feigned, in order to pave the way into the martyrology. This circumstance I will now relate.

While the body was quartered by the executioner, some drops of blood fell upon the straw with which the scaffold was strewed. A man of the name of Wilkinson, who was present, was anxious to preserve some relic of the deceased, and therefore carried home with him some of the straws sprinkled with Garnet's blood. These relics were committed to the care of a woman, who preserved them under a glass case. Wilkinson had come over from St. Omer's on purpose to be present at the execution. It was reported, that the straws which had been carried away by Wilkinson leaped up from the scaffold, or from the basket in which the dissevered head was deposited, upon his person.

Some weeks after, on examining the straws, the parties pretended, that they discovered a likeness of Garnet on one of the husks which contained the grain. Wilkinson and several other persons asserted that they perceived a likeness. The matter was soon noised abroad, and the Romanists proclaimed that a miracle had been wrought. It was thought necessary to institute an examination into the matter; and accordingly several witnesses gave their evidence before the archbishop of Canterbury. Some persons had reported, that the head on the ear of corn was surrounded with *glory*, or with streaming rays; but Griffith, the husband of the woman who had preserved the straw, declared, before the archbishop, that he discovered nothing of the sort, and that the face was no more like Garnet's than that of any other man who had a beard. Another witness deposed, that he believed that a good artisan could have drawn a better likeness.

The matter, however, was not permitted to be forgotten; and at Rome a print of the straw was published and publicly exhibited. Some months afterwards Garnet was declared to be a martyr by the pope; in which light he is still regarded by Romanists. The miracle was undoubtedly intended to afford the pope an excuse for his *beatification*, which is the lowest degree of celestial dignity. "This he did," says Fuller, "to qualify the infamy of Garnet's death, and that the perfume of this new title might outscent the stench of his treason."

The Romanists of that day made the most of this miracle. In a work published soon after, entitled, *The True Christian Catholic*, it is boldly asserted that the sight of Garnet's straw caused at least five hundred persons to embrace the Roman Catholic faith. The miracle was published in all the Romanist states; but in England, it was said, that the man who had been educated at Rome, and commissioned to enter into a conspiracy against his native country, deserved to be pictured in blood.

It appears from Osborne, a contemporary writer, that more than one likeness was pretended. From his statement it seems, that it was circulated, that all the husks in the ears on the straws bore similar impressions of Garnet's features. Osborne says, that he had had some of these straws in his hand; but that he could discover no resemblance to a human face; "yet," says he, "these no doubt are sold and pass at this day for relics, as I know they did twenty years after, and he for a holy saint[23]."

Many false reports were circulated on the Continent respecting his death. It was said that he evinced much readiness to die, whereas he manifested great fear. It was also reported that the people interposed

---

[23] Osborne's *Works*, p. 436.

and prevented the executioner from quartering him while he was alive, but this favour was granted by the command of the king; that the crowd nearly destroyed the hangman, whereas no violence of any sort was used; and that the people were perfectly silent when the head was held up on the scaffold, whereas that act was attended with loud acclamations. On the contrary, the people were with difficulty restrained from taking the law into their own hands, and inflicting summary punishment. The people also understood that Spain and the pope had been plotting with the traitors; and so high was their indignation, that it was necessary for the Spanish ambassador to apply to the government for a guard to protect him from the fury of the populace. These reports were intended to divert attention from his crime, and from the ignominy of his death. That Garnet was a traitor against his sovereign and his country, cannot be denied by any Romanists, without resorting to the usual arts and sophistry of the jesuits, who contrive to deny anything which it may be inconvenient to acknowledge. Yet Bellarmine has defended him on the ground that the treason was revealed in confession: "Why," says he, "was Henry Garnet, a man incomparable for learning in all kinds and holiness of life, put to death, but because he would not reveal that which he could not with a safe conscience?" Garnet, however, as has been shown, acknowledged that he ought to have revealed it; and besides, it was proved on the trial, that he was acquainted with the treason by other means than confession. He admitted that the plot was revealed to him as they were walking, and consequently not under the seal of confession.

The recently discovered papers in the State Paper Office, confirm all the charges advanced against Garnet and the other conspirators at their trial. In these documents there is an account of Garnet's examination. He is asked whether he took Greenwell's discovery of the plot to be in confession or not? he answered, "Not in confession, but by way of confession."

It has already been proved that, by the ancient laws even, it was treason to bring in a bull from Rome; yet Garnet acknowledged that he held three such documents at King James's accession. And on his trial, he justified himself, or rather palliated his offence, by stating, that he had shown them to very few of his own party, when he understood that the king was peaceably put in possession of the throne. He committed the bulls to the flames, but not till he had ascertained that they could not be executed, and that it would be dangerous to retain them, lest they should be discovered in the event of his being taken.

I have already alluded to the mode, in which the continuator of Sir James Mackintosh's *History of England* in *Lardner's Cyclopædia,* writes the history of his country. Another short sentence respecting Garnet, will show how utterly regardless the writer is of truth in his statements: "His guilt or innocence is a question of dispute to this day." He gives a reference to Lingard; but the words are not given as a quotation. Yet Garnet acknowledged his guilt, and it was clearly proved on the trial. Thus, in a history intended for popular use, the guilt of a notorious offender is questioned, and the principles of the church of Rome indirectly defended. The writer further remarks,—"that Garnet's admissions were obtained by the most perfidious and cruel acts of the inquisition; that conviction under the circumstances of his trial, is scarcely a presumption of guilt." This is exactly the strain in which Romanists are accustomed to speak of the plot. In short, the writer has written as a Romanist, and appears to have followed Lingard in every particular. Is such a man qualified to write a history for popular use? But to disprove all his assertions on this point, I simply quote a passage from the *Trial*, which will prove that no cruel means were resorted to in the case of Garnet. In addressing Garnet, the earl of Salisbury said: "You do best know that since your apprehension, even till this day, you have been as Christianly, as courteously, and as carefully used, as ever man could be, of any quality, or any profession; yea, it may truly be said, that you have been as well attended for health or otherwise, as a nurse-child. Is it true or no?" said the earl. "It is most true, my lord," said Garnet, "I confess it." Now, I ask, what dependence can be placed on the continuator of the history in question? Yet such men are employed in the present day to write books for popular use.

CHAPTER VIII.

THE PRINCIPLES ON WHICH THE CONSPIRATORS ACTED.

In this chapter I purpose to give a short account of those principles, on which the conspirators acted, and which were regarded by them as those of their church. I am ready to allow, that many Roman Catholics deprecated the plot and the course taken by the conspirators; but still it is by no means easy to defend the church of Rome from the guilt of the transaction, since she then entertained principles, which appeared to justify the attempt of the parties who were implicated in the treason. That the jesuits were the life and soul of the conspiracy has already been shown in the narrative. They animated the conspirators when they were dispirited,—warranted the proposed action when they were in doubt,—and absolved them from its guilt after the discovery. Nay, they pronounced the deed to be meritorious. They swore them to secresy, and bound them together to the performance of the treason by means of the sacrament. The great wheels, therefore, by which the whole was set in motion, were the jesuits; but the arch-traitor was the pope himself, who had sent his bulls into England, to endeavour to prevent the accession of King James; for it has been shown that the treason originated in those bulls.

I shall *first* briefly state the principles of the church of Rome, on the question of heresy and heretical sovereigns; and *secondly*, examine their practices prior to, and at the period in question, to show how they corresponded exactly with the principles then publicly avowed and defended.

It is an acknowledged principle of the church of Rome, that the decisions of general councils are binding on all. There are disputes amongst her divines respecting some of the councils, whether they were general, or not; but concerning the decisions of those councils which have never been disputed, there is no question with Romanists. Now some of the undisputed councils enforce doctrines at variance with Scripture, and destructive, not merely of the welfare, but of the very existence, of Protestant states and Protestant sovereigns, provided the papal see is sufficiently powerful to carry out her principles into action. No king was completely master in his own dominions, when the papacy was at its height.

The first council to which I refer the reader is *The Third Council of Lateran*, convened by Pope Alexander III., A.D. 1179. Its efforts were directed especially against the Albigenses and Waldenses, who were guilty of no crime, except the unpardonable one of opposing the errors of the church of Rome. Twenty-seven canons were framed by this council; all of them on matters of trivial importance with the exception of the last, which is directed against the poor exiles who were bold enough to prefer their own salvation to a blind submission to the church. The *Twenty-seventh* canon imposes a curse on all those who maintained or favoured the Waldensian opinions. In the event of dying in their alleged errors, they were not even to receive Christian burial[24].

The fourth council of Lateran was held A.D. 1215. One of its canons, the *Third*, is even more horrible than the preceding. All heretics are excommunicated, and delivered over to the secular arm for punishment; while temporal princes are enjoined to extirpate heresy by all means in their power[25]. This exterminating canon is still unrepealed, and may be acted on whenever the church of Rome may have the power to enforce it. It has been attempted in modern times to deny the genuineness of the *Third Canon*; but the attempt was unsuccessful. It has also been pronounced *obsolete*. It is undoubtedly inoperative, simply because the church cannot carry it into execution; but it is still the law of the Roman church.

The council of Constance, A.D. 1415, decided that faith was not to be kept with heretics to the prejudice of the church; and, therefore, John Huss was committed to the flames, in violation of the solemn promise of the emperor.

---

[24] "Although ecclesiastical discipline, being content with the judgment of the priests, does not take sanguinary revenge, yet it is assisted by the decrees of Catholic princes, that men may often seek a saving remedy, through fear of corporal punishment. On this account we decree to subject them (the heretics) and their defenders to anathema: and, under pain of anathema, we forbid that any receive them into his house, or have any dealings with them. Nor let them receive burial among Christians." See the original, *Labb. et Coss.*, Tom. x. 1518-9.

[25] "We excommunicate and condemn every heresy, which exalteth itself against this holy and Catholic Faith. Let such persons, when condemned, be left to the secular powers, to be punished in a fitting manner. And let the secular powers be admonished, and, if need be, compelled, that they should set forth an oath, that to the utmost of their power, they will strive to exterminate all heretics, who shall be denounced by the church. But if any temporal lord shall neglect to cleanse his country of this heretical filth, let him be bound by the chain of excommunication. If he shall scorn to make satisfaction, let it be signified to the supreme pontiff, that he may declare his vassals to be absolved from their fidelity." *Labb. et Coss.* Tom. xi. 147-9. This canon was also received into the *Canon Law*, by Gregory IX. It was carried into effect against the Albigenses.

By these councils all heretics are devoted to destruction. They proclaim principles exactly similar to those on which the conspirators acted;—in other words, the conspirators acted on the principles promulgated by these councils, as those of the church of Rome. On these principles did the jesuits justify the treason, and declare the traitors innocent.

Attempts are made in modern times to prove that the canons alluded to are not binding on the church; but the hand of Providence has made the church of Rome set her seal to her own condemnation in this matter; for by the decrees of the council of Trent every papist is pledged to receive the decisions of all general councils[26]. The only question, therefore, to be decided is this, namely, whether these councils are regarded as *general* by the church of Rome. Respecting the *third* and *fourth* Lateran councils there never was any doubt; and the creed of Pope Pius IV., as well as the council of Trent, expressly enjoins the reception of the decrees of all general councils[27]. It is very remarkable, nay, I may say providential, that the Fourth Lateran council is especially alluded to by the council of Trent. One of the decisions of this very council is specified and renewed by the Trent decrees. The church of Rome has declared, therefore, by her last council,—a council, too, by which all her doctrines were unalterably fixed,—that the Lateran council is to be received by all her members; and, as if to prevent all cavil on the subject, and also to prevent any Romanist from saying that this council was not a general one, and consequently not binding on the church, the council of Trent has expressly designated it a general council. And still further, as if to remove all doubt on the subject, the council of Trent has particularly specified one of the Lateran decrees, by quoting the first two words. The language of the

---

[26] "The holy synod decrees and commends, that the holy canons, and all general councils, and also all constitutions of the Apostolic See, which have been made in favour of ecclesiastical persons and of ecclesiastical liberty, and against the infringers of it, (all of which it revives by this present decree,) be exactly observed by all, as they ought to be." *Conc. Trent.*, Sess. xxv., *De Ref.*, Can. 20. It is observable, too, that emperors and kings are commanded to observe these canons. This is surely a revival of the Lateran canon.

[27] The creed is most explicit on this subject: "I do undoubtedly receive and profess all other things which have been delivered, defined, and declared by the sacred canons, and œcumenical councils, and especially by the holy synod of Trent; and all other things contrary thereto, and all heresies condemned, rejected, and anathematized by the church, I do likewise condemn, reject, and anathematize."

council is remarkable: "All other decrees made by Julius the Third, as also the constitution of Pope Innocent the Third, in a general council, which commences *Qualiter et Quando*, which this holy synod renews, shall be observed by all[28]." Two things are here to be noted. First, the council held under Innocent III. is expressly termed a general council; and this council was the *Fourth Lateran*. Secondly, a particular canon of the council is specified and renewed, so that no doubt can possibly exist as to the particular council to which the reference is made. It is not possible to establish any point with greater precision than this, that the charge of holding persecuting and exterminating doctrines is fastened upon the church of Rome, by these decrees of the council of Trent.

The reader will also perceive that the council of Trent revives and confirms all the constitutions of the apostolic see; that is, all the determinations of the canon law. It would be easy to justify persecution and death from innumerable portions of the canon law. And how can any Romanist allege that the canon law is not binding, when it is expressly confirmed by the council of Trent? It includes all the bulls and decrees of the popes. None of the persecuting decrees have been repealed; and until the church of Rome renounces them by a solemn and public act, she will be obnoxious to the charge of maintaining the duty of persecuting heretics. None of the laws respecting heresy have ever been relaxed; no sovereign was ever censured for punishing heretics; no council has ever relieved the papal sovereigns from the execution of the laws to which I have alluded; nor was any one ever condemned by the head of the church for putting Protestants to death. Until, therefore, Rome repeals her exterminating decrees, she must submit to the heavy charge of maintaining the right to persecute men for their religious belief.

It is well known that the Bull in Cœna Domini is read in the hearing of the pope every Maunday Thursday. By that bull all Protestants are excommunicated and anathematized; and will any one say that the church of Rome would not execute the sentence of excommunication if she possessed the power? To assert the contrary assuredly argues either great obstinacy or egregious folly.

---

[28] *Council of Trent*, sess. xxiv., cap. 5. It is therefore vain for any papist to pretend, in the face of such authority, that there is a doubt whether the Lateran was a general council. In all the editions of the councils it is so designated; it is found in the list of councils appended to the editions of the canon law; and in the canon law itself it is thus reckoned. It is recognised by the council of Constance; and last, though not least, by the council of Trent itself.

To the bull *In Cœna Domini* may be added the oath to the pope taken by every bishop on his elevation to the episcopal dignity, by which he engages to *persecute and attack heretics*.

Such are the principles of the Romish church as embodied in her councils and her canon law. If they are true, then the gunpowder conspirators were justified in their proceedings, nay, they were acting a meritorious part in the prosecution of that design.

Nor have the doctors and eminent supporters of that church hesitated to avow the same principles in days that are past, though in modern times, it has been attempted to deny them, or explain them away. How modern Romanists can consistently deny that such doctrines are enjoined by their church, appears to me inexplicable, except on the jesuitical principle of equivocation, which will enable them to pursue any course calculated to advance the interests of the apostolic see; and though Romanists generally repudiate such doctrines, yet it is asserted in the theology of Dens, and taught at Maynooth, and doubtless in other similar institutions, that heretics are the subjects of the church of Rome[29]. A host of writers might be alleged, who assert that it is lawful to punish heretics with death. So numerous are the passages in Romish authors on this topic, and so well known, that I abstain from any quotations. Still I will meet an objection not unfrequently alleged by Romanists, when pressed in an argument by the authority of names in high repute in their church, namely, that "the church is not bound by the views of particular individuals." The views of these individuals, however, are those of the church, as I have already proved. But further, why are not these views censured if the church does not maintain them? The church of Rome has published an *Index Prohibitorum*, in which all Protestant works are included; and an *Index Expurgatorius*, in which many passages in the works of well known Romanists are marked for erasure as containing sentiments akin to those of the Protestant churches. As, therefore, the church of Rome has not hesitated to expunge passages from the writings of her own members, when she has deemed them at variance with her principles, why, if she views those portions of the works to which I allude, and which enforce the persecution of heretics even to death, to be erroneous, does she not adopt the same process respecting them? As she has not done so, the undoubted inference is, that these writings are

---

[29] Dens. ii. 288. Reiffenstuel quotes the third canon of the fourth Lateran no less than eighteen times in one chapter, and he declares that impenitent heretics are to be put to death. This work is a class-book at Maynooth.

not disapproved of by the church. It is not possible for any Romanist to object to this line of argument; nor can it be charged with unfairness.

Nearly allied to the punishment of heresy is the question of the pope's deposing power. It is asserted in the canons already quoted, and which cannot be disputed; and it is also asserted by numerous writers, whose works have never been censured in an *Index Expurgatorius*. Bellarmine says, "It is agreed upon amongst all, that the pope may lawfully depose heretical princes and free their subjects from yielding obedience to them." Can it be denied, therefore, that such was the doctrine of the church of Rome in the time of Bellarmine? And if such was the doctrine of that church then, it must be the doctrine of the same church now, since none of her articles of faith have been changed, none of her doctrines have been repudiated. It is true that the doctrine is not insisted on by modern Romanists; but what security have we that the claim would not be revived if the church of Rome should ever possess sufficient power to enforce it? We must therefore insist on charging these and similar doctrines on the church of Rome, until she renounces them by a solemn and public decision.

Tillotson's observations on this question, in his sermon on the fifth of November, are so just that I shall make no apology for quoting them. "Indeed, this doctrine hath not been at all times alike frankly and openly avowed; but it is undoubtedly theirs, and hath frequently been put in execution, though they have not thought it so convenient at all times to make profession of it. It is a certain kind of engine, which is to be screwed up or let down as occasion serves: and is commonly kept like Goliah's sword in the sanctuary behind the ephod, but yet so that the high-priest can lend it out upon an extraordinary occasion. And for practices consonant to these doctrines, I shall go no further than the horrid and bloody design of this day."

It is singular that there is no express mention of the deposing power in the council of Trent. The pope and the fathers perceived that times were already altered, that sovereigns were not likely to submit tamely to such an assumption of authority, and that their proceedings must be managed with more craft than formerly. Still the deposing power was established by implication, in the ratification of the decrees of the Lateran council; and we know that it was exercised at a subsequent period against Queen Elizabeth. Parsons declared, in the reign of Queen Elizabeth, that it was the doctrine of all learned men, and agreeable to the apostolic injunctions; and that the power of deposing kings has not only been claimed, but acted upon, may easily be proved. It was not always treated as a speculative doctrine. History shows that many wars have been waged through this very principle. In some cases the papal sentence has been carried into effect, and in others it has led to war and bloodshed, some states having always been ready to attempt to carry the sentence into effect.

The following list will show how frequently the Roman pontiffs in the days of their glory, claimed and exercised the power of deposing sovereigns.

- A.D.
- 1075. Gregory VII. deposed Henry IV. the emperor.
- 1088. Urban II. deposed Philip, king of France.
- 1154. Adrian IV. deposed William, king of Sicily.
- 1198. Innocent III. deposed the Emperor Philip, and King John of England.
- 1227. Gregory IX. deposed the Emperor Frederic II.
- 1242. Innocent IV. deposed the emperor.
- 1261. Urban IV. deposed Manphred, king of Sicily.
- 1277. Nicholas III. deposed Charles, king of Sicily.
- 1281. Martin IV. deposed Peter of Arragon.
- 1284. Boniface VIII. deprived Philip the Fair .
- 1305. Clement V. deposed the Emperor Henry V.
- 1316. John XXII. deprived the Emperor Lodovic.
- 1409. Alexander V. deposed the king of Naples.
- 1538. Paul III. deprived Henry VIII. of England.
- 1570. Pius V. deprived Queen Elizabeth, as did also some of his successors.

This is a sample of papal attempts against kings; and it proves that the popes have always lost sight of St. Peter's character, though acting as his successors. Our own sovereigns have often felt the weight of the papal power. King Edgar was enjoined by Dunstan, the abbot of Glastonbury, not to wear his crown for seven years, to which he was compelled to submit. Henry II. was forced to walk barefooted three miles to visit Becket's shrine, and there to receive fourscore lashes from the monks on his bare back. King John was compelled to resign his crown to the pope's legate, and take it back on condition of paying a yearly sum of a thousand marks to the pope.

The pages of history are pregnant with proofs that, from the period of the Reformation, down to the time when the papacy became shorn of much of its strength, the practices of the church have exactly corresponded with the principles asserted in the canons already specified, in the canon law, and in the works of their eminent writers. I have alluded to the bulls issued against Elizabeth, and to the attempts of nations, and of individuals, to enforce them. Elizabeth escaped; but several continental sovereigns fell a sacrifice to the fury of the church of Rome. Henry III., of France, was murdered in 1589, by a Dominican friar, who was encouraged to the commission of the act by the prior of his convent. Henry was a member of the church of Rome; but he was not so zealous as the pope wished, in executing the laws against heretics. On account, therefore, of his supposed want of zeal, he was devoted to destruction by the church. The deed was lauded in sermons and in books, throughout the French territories; while the murderer, who was destroyed on the spot, was deemed a martyr in the cause of the church. At Rome, the fact was applauded by the pope in a set speech to the cardinals. The act was contrasted by his holiness, with those of Eleazar and Judith, and the palm was given to the friar. Nay, it was compared in greatness to the Incarnation of our Lord Jesus Christ. I give the following extract from this most blasphemous speech:—

"Considering seriously with myself, and applying myself to these things which are now come to pass, I may use the words of the prophet Habbakuk: 'Behold, ye among the heathen, and regard, and wonder marvellously; for I will work a work in your days, which ye will not believe, though it be told you;' i. 5. The French king is slain by the hands of a friar. For unto this it may be compared, though the prophet spake of our Lord's incarnation. This is a memorable and almost incredible thing, not accomplished without the particular providence of God. A friar has killed a king. That the king is dead, is credible; but that he is killed in such a manner is hardly credible: even as we assert that Christ is born of a woman; but if we add of a virgin; then, according to human reason, we cannot assent to it. This great work is to be ascribed to a particular providence."

In this strain did the head of the Roman church laud the murder of Henry III. of France. The deed was reckoned by his holiness as glorious a work as the incarnation of the Saviour, and his resurrection from the dead. Surely, the principles and practices of the church, were in exact correspondence at that time. The principles have never been relinquished; but circumstances control the actions of the church, so that she cannot kill and slay with impunity.

Henry IV. of France also fell a sacrifice to the same principles. He had been an advocate of Protestant doctrines; but from motives of human policy he united himself with the church of Rome. Still, as he did not persecute his Protestant subjects, the sincerity of his conversion was called in question by the church. In less than one month after his public profession of the papal faith, an attempt was made on his life by an assassin, who had been encouraged by the reasonings of certain friars and jesuits. After several escapes, he was stabbed in the street, by a man who had formerly been a monk. His death was not celebrated publicly by the pope, as was that of Henry III., but the jesuits and the friars justified the act, and proved that, on the principles of the church, it was lawful to put him to death, though a Romanist, since he was not zealous against heresy, and in the cause of the papal see. King Henry had also communicated secret information to Cecil, prior to the discovery of the Gunpowder Treason, respecting the machinations of the jesuits and seminary priests. The particulars of their treason were unknown; but the very fact that the French monarch should convey intelligence to King James, was a deadly crime in the eyes of the jesuits. It was supposed at the time, and nothing has since transpired to lead to a different conclusion, that the part he acted, in communicating information to the English court, hastened his tragical end. I have remarked, that the pope did not publicly applaud the act of the assassin; but it is a fact, that his memory was in consequence held in great veneration at Rome, for a considerable period after the event. Henry was supposed to be lukewarm in the cause, and therefore it was determined to remove him out of the way. The assassins of both these monarchs acknowledged, that they were prompted to commit the murders, by the instigation of two jesuits, and the reading of the works of a third.

The massacre of St. Bartholomew is too well known to need the recital of its horrid particulars. I allude to it merely to show how the principles and practices of the church of Rome correspond, whenever she has the power to act. The deed was applauded at Rome, by the head of the church. The crime was consecrated by the pope, who went in grand procession to church, to return thanks to God for so great a blessing as the destruction of the heretics.

It appears that the tidings of the massacre reached Rome on the 6th of September, 1572. The consistory of cardinals was immediately assembled, when the letter from the papal legate, containing the particulars of the massacre, was read. It was immediately determined to repair to the church of St. Mark, where their solemn thanks were offered up to God for this great blessing. Two days after, the pope and cardinals went in procession to the church of Minerva, when high mass was celebrated. The pope also granted a jubilee to all Christendom, and one reason assigned was, *that they should thank God for the slaughter of the enemies of the church, lately executed in France*. Two days later, the cardinal of Lorraine headed another great procession of cardinals, clergy, and ambassadors, to the chapel of St. Lewis, where he himself celebrated mass. In the name of the king of France, the cardinal thanked the pope and the cardinals, for the aid they had afforded his majesty by their counsels and prayers, of which he had experienced the happy effects. On his own part, and on the part of the church, the pope sent a legate to thank the king for his zeal in the extirpation of the heretics, and to beseech him to persevere in the great and holy work. The legate, in passing through France, gave a plenary absolution to all who had been actors in the massacre. On the evening of the day on which the news arrived at Rome, the guns were fired from the castle of St. Angelo; and the same rejoicings were practised as were common on receiving the intelligence of an important victory. The pope looked upon the massacre, as one of the greatest felicities which could have happened at the beginning of his papacy.

In addition to these public rejoicings on the part of the pope and his cardinals at Rome, other means were adopted to indicate the sense of the church on the massacre. Medals were struck to commemorate the event. On the one side was a representation of the slaughter, an angel cutting down the heretics, and on the other, the head of the pope, Gregory XIII. On these medals, was this inscription, *"Ugonottorum Strages, 1572."* The slaughter was also deemed worthy of being commemorated on tapestry, which was placed in the pope's chapel. In the paintings which were executed, the slaughter of the Huguenots was depicted, *"Colignii et Sociorum cædes;"* and in another part, *"Rex Colignii cædam probat."*

Let it be remembered that the principles of the church of Rome are unchanged, and, as the Romanists themselves aver, unchangeable. The circumstances of Europe are widely different from what they were in the sixteenth century; and Romanists themselves are under the restraint of wholesome laws and public opinion; but were the popes of modern days to be supported by sovereigns like Charles IX. of France, or were they possessed of the same power as was once enjoyed by their predecessors, is it reasonable to suppose, that the principles which are still retained, would not be carried out into practice; or that the same scenes, which then disgraced the civilized world, would not again be enacted in every country, in which the jesuits and other active emissaries of the papacy could obtain a footing?

Is it not clear from the preceding facts, that the murderers of Henry III. and IV. and the actors in the massacre of St. Bartholomew considered that they were acting a meritorious part? They were taught that the pope could depose kings and grant their kingdoms to others; and they knew that the pope had often exercised that power. The Gunpowder conspirators were men of the same class and influenced by the same views. Knowing that all heretics are annually excommunicated, they believed that they were authorized to carry the sentence into effect; and having been taught that heretical princes might lawfully be deposed, they considered themselves at liberty to attempt their destruction. The assassins of the French monarchs and the Gunpowder traitors, being encouraged by the authority of the church, as explained by their spiritual directors, entered upon their deeds of darkness, with an assurance, that they were merely obeying the commands of their ghostly fathers.

The pope endeavoured to clear himself from the guilt of being privy to the Gunpowder Treason; yet some of the planners and contrivers of the plot were protected at Rome. Had his holiness been sincere in his professions to King James, he would have delivered up those jesuits who were implicated in the treason, and who escaped to Rome. The surrender of the conspirators would have been the strongest proof of his sincerity. But not only did he not give them up to the sovereign, whose life they had sought; he did not even call them to account for the part which they had taken in the conspiracy. I would not charge the guilt of that conspiracy on the members of the church of Rome indiscriminately, for there were many who were horror-struck at the deed, and there always have been many who did not receive all the principles maintained by the church; but I contend, that the head of the church, the pope of that day, approved of the act, or he would never have adopted the course which he then pursued; and in his guilt all the leading members of the conclave were also implicated. We can only judge of men by their actions; which, if they mean any thing, certainly involve the church of Rome of that period in the guilt of the treason. Garnet was regarded as a martyr, not as a traitor; and the absurd miracle of the *Straw*, was sanctioned at Rome. These facts certainly involve the then church of Rome in the treason; and as her principles are unchanged, there would be no security against the same practices, were circumstances to favour her ascendency[30].

It is also worthy of remark, that the jesuits who were privy to the design, and who escaped from the knife of the executioner, never expressed the least remorse for the part they had taken; on the contrary, they never failed to speak of the treason as a glorious and meritorious deed. When Hall the jesuit, *alias* Oldcorne, was reminded of the ill success of the treason as a proof that it was displeasing to God, he immediately replied, that the justice of the cause must not be determined by the event, for that the eleven tribes were commanded by God himself to fight against Benjamin, and were twice overthrown; and that Lewis of France was conquered by the Turks. By reminding some of his dispirited companions of many glorious enterprises, which had failed in the first instance, he hoped to encourage them to persevere, and to induce them to expect that God would, in the end, enable them

---

[30] Hallam remarks, "There seems, indeed, some ground for suspicion, that the Nuncio at Brussels was privy to the conspiracy; though this ought not to be asserted as an historical fact." *Const. Hist.* i. 554.

to accomplish their purposes. Who can deny, after these facts, that the church of Rome was deeply involved in the gunpowder treason? Or who can exculpate her, even at present, from the charge of maintaining principles subversive of Christian liberty and Protestant governments? When one of the conspirators, who was received by the governor of Calais, was condoled with, on being banished his country, he replied, "It is the least part of our grief that we are banished our native country; this doth truly and heartily grieve us, that we could not bring so generous and wholesome a design to perfection."

Sir Everard Digby was a mild and amiable man, and, with the exception of his participation in the plot, no stain rests upon his character; yet he seems to have considered that, by engaging in this treason, he was really doing God service. His letters, written during his imprisonment, and published by Bishop Barlow in 1679, illustrate the influence of the principles of the church of Rome on the mind of an otherwise excellent individual. They were written with the juice of lemon, or something of the same kind: written, too, when he had time to reflect in his solitary cell, yet it is evident that he thought he was advancing the cause of true religion in the part which he took; and, further, that he was never convinced that the deed was sinful, so completely had the jesuitical principles of the prime actors in the conspiracy warped his judgment and influenced his views. The papers were discovered in the house of Charles Cornwallis, Esq., who was the executor of Sir Kenelm Digby, the son and heir of Sir Everard. They were once in the possession of Archbishop Tillotson, as he testifies in one of his sermons.

The letters were by some secret means conveyed to his lady, and were preserved in the family as sacred relics. "Sir Everard Digby," says Archbishop Tillotson in his sermon on the fifth of November, "whose very original papers and letters are now in my hands, after he was in prison, and knew he must suffer, calls it the best cause, and was extremely troubled to hear it censured by Catholics and priests, contrary to his expectations, for a great sin." The letters were also, once in the possession of Bishop Burnet, as he himself informs us. From him we learn how they were discovered. "The family being ruined upon the death of Sir Kenelm's son, when the executors were looking out for writings to make out the titles of the estates they were to sell, they were directed by an old servant to a cupboard that was very artificially hid, in which some papers lay that she had observed *Sir Kenelm* was oft reading. They, looking into it, found a velvet bag, within which, there were two other silk bags, (so carefully were those relics kept) and there was within these a collection of all the letters that *Sir Everard* writ during his imprisonment."

A few extracts will show what his sentiments were concerning the plot.

"Now, for my intention let me tell you, that if I had thought there had been the least sin in the plot, I would not have been of it for all the world; and no other cause drew me to hazard my fortune and life, but zeal to God's religion. For my keeping it secret, it was caused by certain belief, that those which were best able to judge of the lawfulness of it, had been acquainted with it, and given way unto it."

"Now, let me tell you, what a grief it hath been to me, to hear that so much condemned, which I did believe would have been otherwise thought on by Catholics."

"Oh! how full of joy should I die, if I could do any thing for the cause which I love more than my life."

On the proceedings which were to have been adopted in the event of the success of the plot, Sir Everard remarks:

"There was also a course taken to have given present notice to all princes, and to associate them with an oath, answerable to the league in France."

Respecting the pope's concurrence he has the following passage:

"Before that I knew any thing of the plot, I did ask Mr. Farmer, what the meaning of the pope's brief was: he told me that they were not (meaning priests) to undertake or procure stirs; but yet they would not hinder any, neither was it the pope's mind they should, that should be undertaken for Catholic good. I did never utter thus much, nor would not but to you; and this answer, with Mr. Catesby's proceedings with him and me, gave me absolute belief that the matter in general was approved, though every particular was not known."

Then alluding to the presence of some Romanist peers at the opening of parliament, he adds:

"I do not think there would have been three worth saving that should have been lost."

In another letter he observes:

"I could give unanswerable reasons, both for the good that this would have done for the Catholic cause, and my being from home, but I think it now needless, and for some respects unfit."

The last letter is a long one, and is addressed to his sons; but though he exhorts them to continue in the faith of the church of Rome, yet he does not express any sorrow for his crime; nor does he caution them against being engaged in similar conspiracies. It is, therefore, clear, that he viewed the deed as laudable and meritorious, even at the close of his career.

It appears certain that many of the Romanists, both at home and abroad, were aware that some extensive conspiracy was on foot. A particular prayer was used, it is said, by numbers in England, for the success of the conspiracy; it was couched in the following terms: "Prosper, Lord, their pains, that labour in thy cause day and night; let heresy vanish like smoke; let the memory of it perish with a crack, like the ruin and fall of a broken house." It would appear that this prayer was framed by one who was privy to the conspiracy; nor can it be doubted that it was intended to convey some intimation of the nature of the treason. I am, aware, that no Romanist would in the present day justify the deed; but the preceding facts prove, that the act was applauded and justified at the time by the whole church almost, and for a considerable period afterwards. To justify the treason now, would be to expose the parties who did so, to the execration of an indignant public. The principles of Rome, however, are exactly what they were when the bulls of the pope were sent to Garnet, and when the gunpowder treason was planned. Tillotson forcibly observes, "I would not be understood to charge every particular person, who is, or hath been in the Roman communion, with the guilt of those or the like practices; but I must charge their doctrines and principles with them. I must charge the heads of their church, and the prevalent teaching and governing part of it, who are usually the contrivers and abettors, the executioners and applauders of these cursed designs[31]."

It was decided by Pope Urban II. that it was neither treason nor murder to kill those, who were excommunicated by the church. So that any treason or murder could be justified on such principles. Nor has any change been effected in the principles of the church of Rome. "Popery," says Burnet, "cannot change its nature, and *cruelty and breach of faith to heretics*, are as necessary parts of that religion, as *transubstantiation* and the *pope's supremacy*[32]." Andrew Marvel wittily remarks of the pope's claim, "He has, indeed, of late, been somewhat more retentive than formerly as to his faculty of disposing of kingdoms, the thing not having succeeded well with him in some instances, but he lays the same claim still, continues the same inclinations, and though velvet-headed hath the more itch to be pushing. And, however, in order to any occasion he keeps himself in breath, always by cursing one prince or other upon every Maundy Thursday[33]."

---

[31] Tillotson's *Works*, 12mo., Vol. i., 349.
[32] Burnet's *Eighteen Papers*, 84.
[33] *The Growth of Popery*, p. 9.

CHAPTER IX.

THE ACT FOR THE OBSERVANCE OF THE DAY—A SERVICE
PREPARED FOR THE OCCASION—ALTERATIONS IN THE
SERVICE TO SUIT THE LANDING OF KING WILLIAM—
REFLECTIONS.

As the Act of Parliament which enjoins the observance of the
Fifth of November is not generally known, or at all events is not within
the reach of ordinary readers, I shall insert in this place. It was couched
in the following terms:—

"Forasmuch as Almighty God hath in all ages shewed his power
and mercy, in the miraculous and gracious deliverance of his Church,
and in the protection of religious kings and states, and that no nation of
the earth hath been blessed with greater benefits than this nation now
enjoyeth, having the true and free profession of the Gospel under our
most gracious Sovereign Lord King James, the most great, learned, and
religious king that ever reigned therein, enriched with a most hopeful
and plentiful progeny, proceeding out of his royal loins, promising
continuance of this happiness and profession to all posterity: the which
many malignant and devilish papists, jesuits, and seminary priests,
much envying and fearing, conspired most horribly when the king's
most excellent majesty, the queen, the prince, and all the lords spiritual
and temporal, and commons, should have been assembled in the Upper
House of Parliament upon the Fifth day of November, in the year of our
Lord 1605, suddenly to have blown up the said whole house with
gunpowder: an invention so inhuman, barbarous, and cruel, as the like
was never before heard of, and was (as some of the principal
conspirators thereof confess) purposely devised and concluded to be
done in the said house, that when sundry necessary and religious laws
for preservation of the church and state were made, which they falsely
and slanderously call cruel laws, enacted against them and their
religion, both place and person should be all destroyed and blown up at
once, which would have turned to the utter ruin of this whole kingdom,
had it not pleased Almighty God, by inspiring the king's most excellent
majesty with a divine spirit, to interpret some dark phrases of a letter
shewed to his majesty, above and beyond all ordinary construction,
thereby miraculously discovering this hidden treason not many hours
before the appointed time for the execution thereof: therefore the king's
most excellent majesty, the lords spiritual and temporal, and all his
majesty's faithful and loving subjects, do most justly acknowledge this
great and infinite blessing to have proceeded merely from God his great
mercy, and to his most holy name do ascribe all honour, glory, and

praise: and to the end this unfeigned thankfulness may never be forgotten, but be had in a perpetual remembrance, that all ages to come may yield praises to his Divine Majesty for the same, and have in memory this joyful day of deliverance:

"Be it therefore enacted, by the king's most excellent majesty, the lords spiritual and temporal, and the commons in this present parliament assembled, and by the authority of the same, that all and singular ministers in every cathedral, and parish-church, or other usual place for common prayer, within this realm of England, and the dominions of the same, shall always upon the Fifth day of November say morning prayer, and give unto Almighty God thanks for this most happy deliverance: and that all and every person and persons inhabiting within this realm of England, and the dominions of the same, shall always upon that day diligently and faithfully resort to the parish-church or chapel accustomed, or to some usual church or chapel, where the said morning prayer, preaching, or other service of God, shall be used, and then and there to abide orderly and soberly during the time of the said prayers, preaching, or other service of God there to be used and ministered.

"And because all and every person may be put in mind of his duty, and be there better prepared to the said holy service, be it enacted by the authority aforesaid, that every minister shall give warning to his parishioners, publicly in the church at morning prayer, the Sunday before every such Fifth day of *November*, for the due observation of the said day. And that after morning prayer or preaching on the said Fifth day of *November*, they read publicly, distinctly, and plainly, the present Act[34]."

A particular service was prepared to be used on the Fifth of November, and was published in 1606. I have not been able to ascertain whether it was framed by the convocation; but I am disposed to think that it was arranged by the bishops, as is still the case in particular prayers on special occasions, and then set forth by the authority of the crown. In my copy of the original service printed by Barker and Bill, printers to the king, the words "Set forth by authority," stand on the title-page. The authority of the crown is evidently intended, and not that of convocation.

The original service was used on this day until the alterations were effected in 1662, except during the period of the Commonwealth, when forms of prayer were altogether discarded. It appears, however,

---

[34] I give the Act entire, because I am not aware that it is to be found in any popular form; and it is desirable that the present generation should know how this treason was viewed by their ancestors.

from Fuller, that in his time, the observance of the day was very much neglected. "If this plot," says he, "had taken effect, the papists would have celebrated this day with all solemnity; and it would have taken the upper hand of all other festivals. The more, therefore, the shame and pity, that amongst Protestants the keeping of this day (not yet full fifty years old) begins already to wax weak and decay; so that the red letters, wherever it is written, seem to grow dimmer and paler in our English calendar. God forbid that our thankfulness for this great deliverance, formerly so solemnly observed, should hereafter be like the *squibs* which the apprentices in London make on this day; and which give a great flash and crack at first, but soon go out in a stink[35]."

This was written, or, at all events, the work was published, during the Commonwealth; and it would seem that the various religious parties of the period, though hostile to popery, did not pay much attention to the observance of the day, probably because it had been set apart as a holy day by the church of England. The fact that the day was observed by the Anglican church, was quite sufficient to induce the presbyterians and sectaries to disregard it. On no other ground can I account for the omission or neglect of which Fuller speaks; for the religious parties of that period, were all animated with feelings of the bitterest hostility towards the church of Rome.

After the restoration, the day was again solemnly observed in all the churches of the kingdom; and when the Book of Common Prayer was revised and set forth, the service for the Fifth of November was revised also, and published with the Liturgy. The original service was submitted to the convocation, by whom several alterations were made, which may be seen by comparing the service published in 1606 with that which is annexed to the Common Prayer subsequent to 1662, and which continued in that state until after the Revolution. The title of the original service is, *"Prayers and Thanksgiving to be used by all the King's Majestie's loving Subjects, for the happy deliverance of his Majesty, the Queen, Prince, and States of Parliament, from the most traiterous and bloody intended massacre by gunpowder, the 5 of November, 1605."* In the service as it was revised in 1662, some few

---

[35] Fuller, book x. 38. From several of the incidental notices in the works of writers of the times of James I. and Charles I., we learn that the observance of the day was gradually neglected. In a curious work of the date of 1618, there is a notice to the effect that the people were cold in praising God for their deliverance. See Garey's *Amphitheatrum Scelerum.* 4to. 1618. In the reigns of Charles II. and James II., when the dread of popery was general, the people universally observed the Fifth of November as a day of thanksgiving to God.

alterations were made in the title. They may be seen by any one, who compares the above with the title in the service at present in use, for in this particular it has undergone no change since 1662. In the commencement of the original service are two verses from 1 Timothy ii. 1, 2: in the revised form of 1662 they are omitted. The rubrics, also, in the service of 1662, respecting the method to be adopted when the day falls upon a Sunday or holy-day, are not found in the service of 1606. The psalms appointed to be read are also different in the two services. In the service as altered in 1662, and as it stands at present, one of the homilies against rebellion is appointed to be read, whenever there is no sermon, while in that of 1606, no mention is made of anything of the kind[36].

The service of 1662, like the original, was framed to commemorate one event only, namely, the deliverance from the gunpowder plot; but when King William came to the throne, it was deemed desirable, as he had landed on the same day, to commemorate that event also. It became necessary, therefore, to alter the service so as to make it suit both events; *first*, the deliverance from the gunpowder treason; and *secondly*, the deliverance of the country from popish tyranny and superstition by the arrival of King William. It has been supposed, that the service was altered into its present state by the convocation in 1689; but there is no evidence to prove that such was the case. It seems pretty certain that it was altered by the authority of the crown. A twofold deliverance, therefore, is commemorated in the present *service* for the Fifth of November; *first*, from the powder plot, and *next*, from popery coming in upon the country in a manner more insidious, but not less dangerous in 1688, when the king on the throne was a papist, and all possible means were used to establish the papal ascendancy.

It was very natural, that the country should have been struck with the circumstance of King William's landing on the Fifth of November,—a day so remarkable in the calendar of the English church. To the Roman Catholics the observance of this day is anything but agreeable; but they can scarcely censure Englishmen for commemorating an event so favourable to Protestantism. Had such a conspiracy been discovered against the church of Rome, all papists would regard the day with special reverence. Protestants are surely to be permitted to enjoy the same liberty, in celebrating the merciful interposition of Providence in rescuing the country from destruction.

---

[36] I notice these alterations, because the original service is very rare, and consequently accessible only to a few.

By some modern writers, the *Revolution* of 1688 is designated a *Rebellion*! It is astonishing, that any Protestant should speak of that event in such terms; since Queen Victoria must be an usurper, if the revolution was a rebellion. To the principles then established, our queen is indebted for her crown; and we are indebted to the same principles, for our civil and religious liberties. The men, who can call the revolution a rebellion, cannot be members of the church of England; for had not King James been expelled from the throne, the Anglican church would have been destroyed. Rebellions can never be lawful; but revolutions, similar to that in 1688, are perfectly just. Such men can never read the Service appointed for the *Fifth of November*; at all events, they cannot read the following passages:—"Accept also, most gracious God, of our unfeigned thanks, for filling our hearts again with joy and gladness, after the time that thou hadst afflicted us, and putting a new song into our mouths, by bringing his majesty King *William*, upon this day, for the deliverance of our church and nation from popish tyranny and arbitrary power." And again, "And didst likewise upon this day, wonderfully conduct thy servant King *William*, and bring him safely into *England*, to preserve us from the attempts of our enemies to bereave us of our religion and laws." And the following, "We bless thee for giving his late majesty King *William* a safe arrival here, and for making all opposition fall before him, till he became our king and governor." It is not possible that the men, who can call the revolution a rebellion, should concur in those prayers. Had these individuals lived at the time, they would have quitted the church with the nonjurors; and with such views, respecting the revolution settlement, I cannot conceive how they can conscientiously remain in a church connected with, and supported by a government which owes its very existence to that event, which they designate a rebellion. Is it not high time for such men to quit the pale of the Anglican church?

The dangers which threatened the country during the reign of James II. were very great; and their removal can only be ascribed to Him, in whose hands are the issues of life. James was determined to reduce the country into subjection to the papal see, or lose all in the attempt. William III. was the destined instrument under God, to secure the liberties, which James laboured with all his might to destroy. The revolution of 1688 was a bloodless one; yet it was complete. It is always dangerous to alter the succession to the crown; it is a expedient never to be resorted to except in extreme danger. In 1688, the departure from the direct line was an act of necessity; for unless such a course had been adopted, the liberties of England, both temporal and spiritual, would have been sacrificed. Nor can any one say how long the country would have been in recovering them from the grasp of the papacy. In such an emergency the nation looked to the prince of Orange, who responded to the call, and came to our rescue. When King James quitted the country, and all hope of his being prevailed upon to govern justly was lost, the people saw the necessity of departing from the direct line of succession. Still they were resolved to depart as little as possible. They looked therefore to the next Protestant heir, being determined to exclude papists from the throne for ever. That *heir* was the princess of Orange, the daughter of King James; and as the prince had been so instrumental in rescuing the nation from the yoke, he was associated with her in the government. James, therefore, would not have been rejected if he had governed righteously; but when he had deserted the throne, it was determined that it should never again be filled with a papist. Such were the principles on which the revolution was conducted.

When the prince of Orange set sail from Holland, he was driven back by contrary winds; and it was feared that the attempt would fail, and that King James would succeed in his designs. A second time, however, were the sails unfurled, and a propitious wind bore the fleet to the coast of Devon, where a landing was effected on the Fifth of November, 1688.

The Fifth of November, 1605, and the Fifth of November, 1688, are remarkable days in the annals of England—days never to be forgotten by a grateful people. Had not the prince of Orange arrived, James would have imposed his yoke upon the English nation. Had he not been resisted, the laws and liberties of the country must have been prostrated in the dust, and the church of England sacrificed to popery.

King James, as a papist, felt himself bound to make every effort to restore popery, and root out Protestantism. All his actions tended to this point. Motives of policy even did not restrain him in the course upon which he had entered. His proceedings, therefore, were against the liberties of the people, and the laws of the land; and on this account alone was he set aside. The parliament acted as a Protestant parliament, and enacted a law, that none but a Protestant should ever occupy the British throne. The parliament of that day well knew that the same principles would be productive of similar results, and that Protestantism, and the civil liberties of the nation, would be endangered by a popish king. Now, had not King William arrived, James would have been able to execute all his projects respecting the church and nation; so that every Protestant has reason to be thankful for the success, which attended the efforts of William III., and to observe the *Fifth of November* as a day of thanksgiving to God for his gracious interposition.

Never was a people less disposed to rise against their sovereign than were the English against James II. Yet, as he was trampling upon their liberties, and preparing a yoke of spiritual bondage, what could they do? Their rights as men and as Christians were at stake; nor could the danger by which they were threatened, be averted, but by the expulsion of that sovereign, who had broken his solemn promise, and proved himself unworthy of being trusted again by his subjects. Our ancestors at the period of the revolution, acted on the principle of self-defence. It was necessary to deprive him of his royal power, when that power would have been employed in depriving the people of their civil and religious liberties.

It was admitted by an illustrious statesman in France, in the seventeenth century, that it was the true interest of England to maintain and defend her Protestant church against popery. As his observations are so striking, and also so applicable to our present circumstances, I shall not hesitate to quote them. The book bears this title, *The Interest of the Princes and States of Christendom*, and consists of several chapters, in each of which he treats of *The Interest* of a particular country. There is a chapter on *The Interest of England*, from which I quote the following passages: "Queen Elizabeth (who by her prudent government hath equalled the greatest kings of Christendom), knowing well the disposition of her state, believed that the true interest thereof consisted, *first* in holding a firm union in itself, deeming (as it is most true) that *England is a mighty animal, which can never die except it kill itself.* She grounded this fundamental maxim, *to banish thence the exercise of the Roman religion,* as the only means to break all the plots of the *Spaniards,* who under this pretext, did there foment rebellion." Alluding to some other particulars of that reign he adds:—"By all these maxims, this wise princess has made known to her successors that besides the interest which the king of England has with all princes, he has yet one *particular*, which is that, *he ought* thoroughly to acquire the advancement of the Protestant religion, even with as much zeal as the King of Spain appears protector of the Catholic." This was the language of a statesman. King James, therefore, did not seek the *interest* of his country, but *that* of the papacy[37].

A few words will suffice to shew that King James intended to subvert the liberties of his subjects, to root out Protestantism, and to re-establish popery.

In his first speech to his parliament, he promised to support the church of England as by law established; yet, two days after his

---

[37] See *The Interest of the Princes and States of Christendom, by the Duke De Rohan, translated into English by H. H.* Page 53, 12mo. 1641.

accession, he went publicly to mass. The very same year he appointed several popish officers to posts in the army, in direct violation of the statute passed in the late reign on this subject. In 1686, he endeavoured to induce the twelve judges to declare the legality of the *dispensing power*. While under the direction of a jesuit, his confessor, a majority of papists were introduced into his council; and at the same period several popish bishops were publicly consecrated in St. James's Chapel, contrary to the laws of the land. Many of his nobles were removed from their offices of trust and honour, simply for refusing to embrace popery, while the clergy were commanded not to introduce controversial topics into their sermons; and because Sharp, subsequently archbishop of York, refused to comply with the royal order, he was prosecuted in the courts of justice, and his diocesan, the bishop of London, was actually suspended for refusing to censure him contrary to law. In 1687, under the pretence of relieving the dissenters, he dispensed with the penal laws, in order that popery might be propagated under cover of a toleration. In 1688, seven bishops were committed to the Tower, for no other crime than that of petitioning his majesty in favour of the civil and religious liberties of the country. At length, when the king's designs were obvious to all men, the prince of Orange was applied to by the general consent of the English nation. That great prince responded to the call, and, after some little delay at sea, landed on our shores on the Fifth of November, 1688, and completed the deliverance of the country from the yoke of bondage. Well, therefore, may this event be coupled with the deliverance of this nation from the Gunpowder Treason of 1605.

It must strike the reader as very strange, that in matters of religion, we should not be left at liberty to act for ourselves, without the interference of the pope and the Roman church. This very fact shows, that her claim of supremacy is an essential part of her system. The church of England, the papists allege, has made a departure from the church of Christ. This would be a grievous charge, if it could be proved. The church of Christ commands nothing but what is comformable to the Saviour's will; nor does she require her children to believe anything, which is not expressly contained in the Scriptures, or by evident consequence deduced from those sacred oracles. It is, therefore, false to assert, that the church of England has made a separation from the church of Christ. She merely opposes those dogmas, which cannot be proved from sacred scripture. So far from separating from the church of Christ, she did not even separate from the church of Rome. The church of England, in a lawful synod, assembled early in the reign of Queen Elizabeth, declared certain opinions, which were held by some in her communion, to be contrary to the word of

God. This power the church of England ever possessed; and ages before the Reformation she had often exercised it. This power had been wrested from the church of England by force; and at the Reformation she recovered it. William the Conqueror, and many of his successors, though sons of the Roman church, yet acted as independently as Queen Elizabeth. For ages our kings did not permit letters to be received from Rome without being submitted to their inspection: they did not permit any councils to be held without their permission; so that ecclesiastical councils were at length termed convocations, and were always assembled by the authority of the crown. They did not permit any synodical decree to take effect, but with their concurrence, and confirmation. Bishops could not excommunicate any baron or great officer without the royal precept; or if they did, they were called to account for their conduct in the courts of law. They never permitted a legate from the pope to enter England, but by express consent; nor did they suffer appeals to Rome, as was the case when the encroachments of the papacy were further advanced. Frequently they would not permit bishops to be confirmed in their sees by the pope, but commanded the archbishop of Canterbury to give possession to the individuals appointed to fill them. These are a few instances in which our kings in ancient times exercised a power in ecclesiastical affairs independent of the pope; and, therefore, Queen Elizabeth had a full right to act as her predecessors had done for so many ages. The same power had been possessed and exercised by every national church from the earliest times. She proceeded, therefore, to correct abuses; and the pope and his followers, without even examining the matter, and setting at nought the ancient privileges of the kingdom, designated this procedure a departure from the church. The pope wished to impose, as articles of belief, certain doctrines, which had no foundation in Scripture: the English church refused to receive them; and the pope condemned us as schismatics and heretics. Yet, in all reason those who depart from the Bible, not those who adhere to it, must be the heretics. To impose these same articles of belief the Gunpowder Treason was planned! To impose the same, James II. resorted to those means, which are so well known as having caused him the loss of his crown. To commemorate our deliverance from such an authority—from such a yoke of bondage—and from such cruel tyranny, the Fifth of November was ordered by act of parliament to be for ever kept holy. That act is still in force; and I am convinced that it will remain in force; for no minister of the crown, however inclined to favour and conciliate the Papists, will ever be so rash as to call for a repeal of that act. Such an attempt would rouse the Protestant feeling of the empire: it would be viewed as a precursor of the complete ascendency of popery. I am convinced that the repeal of the act, if such a thing were carried, would cause the Protestants of England to observe the day with more solemnity than has ever been practised since the passing of the act. Our churches would be opened for worship; our pulpits would resound with the full declaration of the truths of our holy religion against the devices and the corruptions of popery; and the loud song of praise and thanksgiving would be offered up from England's twelve thousand parishes, with such ardour and devotional zeal, that no attempt to crush the expression of public feeling would succeed. If, therefore, a popishly affected ministry should ever venture to repeal the act, they will be under the necessity, if they would repress the demonstration of popular feeling, of passing another act to prevent the doors of our churches from being opened, and the people from assembling together to praise God on the "Fifth of November."

In alluding to the observance of the day, Burnet remarks, "Now our Fifth of November is to be enriched by a second service, since God has ennobled it so far, as to be the beginning of that which we may justly hope shall be our complete deliverance from all plots and conspiracies; and that this second day shall darken, if not quite wear out the former[38]." To us in the present day both deliverances may be recalled with equal advantage. Both were wonderful! Both demand a tribute of gratitude from all who love the religion of the Bible. Burnet observes in the same sermon, "You who saw the state of things three months ago, could never have thought that so total a revolution could have been brought about so easily as if it had been only the shifting of scenes. These are speaking instances to let you see of what consequence it is to a nation to have the Lord for its God. We have seen it hitherto in so eminent a manner, that we are forced to conclude that we are under a special influence of heaven: and since in God there is no variableness, nor shadow of turning, we must confess that, if there comes any change in God's methods towards us, it arises only out of our ingratitude and unworthiness." He then states that, if the advantages so conferred are not duly appreciated and improved, more dreadful calamities than those lately expected will overtake the country. When addressing the Commons on their duties relative to religious matters, he tells them that one important duty is, "to secure us for ever, as far as human wisdom and the force of law can do it, from ever falling under the just apprehensions of the return of idolatry any more amongst us,

---

[38] Burnet's *Thanksgiving Sermon before the Commons, Jan. 31, 1688-1689.*

and the making the best provision possible against those dangers that lay on us so lately[39]."

I am disposed to think, that the act of parliament by which the observance of the day is enjoined, is not read, in the present day, in our churches: some of the clergy have never even seen it. The present work is intended to call the attention of churchmen, and especially of the clergy, to this important subject. Should I be assured, that any of my brethren have been led, by the perusal of this volume, to regard the day with more solemnity than usual, I shall feel myself amply recompensed for my labours. At the period of the Revolution, and for many years after, the act, as we learn from incidental notices of contemporary writers, was always read by the clergy from the pulpits. The people were then fully sensible of the deliverance, which had been completed on that day; while the clergy invariably directed the attention of their parishioners to the subject; and both clergy and people presented their tribute of gratitude to that gracious Being from whom all good things proceed. And why should the present generation be less mindful of the great deliverance than their ancestors? We have just as much reason to be thankful as the men of that generation; for if the papists had succeeded in their designs, not only would the liberties of that age have been sacrificed, but those also of succeeding periods. May the Protestants of this kingdom never be forgetful of the glorious Arm by which our salvation from papal thraldom and error was alone effected! It is generally allowed that a retrospection into the transactions of past ages is as a glass, in which the clearest view of future events may be obtained: for, by comparing things together, we shall arrive at this conclusion, that men of the same principles will always, either directly or indirectly, aim at the same ends. The end, which all Romanists have in view, is the destruction of the church of England as the greatest bulwark of Protestantism. In past ages this end was sought to be accomplished directly by treason and murder; in the present day the end is attempted by secret means, by an affectation of moderation, and by an avowal of sentiments which are not in reality maintained. Let Protestants ever bear in mind, that the same causes will generally produce the same effects, though the means employed may be varied according to times and circumstances. Ever since the revolution in 1688, popery, in this country, has worn a mask; but the papal party are now venturing to cast it aside, and to appear in their real character. Within the last few years scenes have been exhibited in this Protestant land, which our ancestors would never for one moment have tolerated. Many Protestants are lukewarm amid these ominous proceedings. May

---

[39] Ibid. pp. 31, 32.

they be aroused from their present apathy into a spirit worthy of the men, by whom our deliverance from papal tyranny was effected in One Thousand Six Hundred and Eighty-Eight.

www.ingramcontent.com/pod-product-compliance
Lightning Source LLC
Chambersburg PA
CBHW052159090426
42741CB00010B/2337